Praise for *Decolonizing Wealth*, Second Edition

"If we are to escape the insidious hold racism has on our society, we must be intentional about truth and reconciliation. In *Decolonizing Wealth*, Edgar lays a foundation that not only explains the history of wealth and racism but also provides a pathway to healing that we all need."
—**Ibram X. Kendi, National Book Award–winning author of *Stamped from the Beginning* and *How to Be an Antiracist***

"Only a truthful reckoning of our history of colonization can inform the transformation of our extractive economic systems. Recognition, repair, and transformation are not only moral imperatives—but they will also finally and truly benefit us all. Edgar knows this deeply and is leading the way."
—**Kat Taylor, philanthropist and cofounder of Beneficial State Bank**

"Due to years of detrimental federal Indian policy and discriminatory economic systems, Native American communities have been marginalized and left out of the economic opportunity experienced by other Americans. Edgar offers a new vision and an Indigenous perspective that can put us on a better path. Everyone should read *Decolonizing Wealth*, especially those who control the flow of resources in government, philanthropy, and finance."
—**LaDonna Harris (Comanche), politician, activist, and founder of Americans for Indian Opportunity**

"*Decolonizing Wealth* is a call to action for all who seek real, meaningful progress. If we want to see the kinds of change, unity, and radical generosity that we know are possible, we must reckon with the systems that continue to perpetuate the racial wealth gap and change them from the root up. We need healing, we need hope, we need solidarity, and in this book, Edgar has provided the blueprint."
—**Asha Curran, CEO of GivingTuesday**

"Edgar is an incredible thinker and activist. His work is fueling efforts across the globe to face necessary truths about history and to take reparative actions. Everyone should read this book to understand mutual liberation and the powerful and necessary ways that we can heal ourselves, our communities, and our world."
—**Matt McGorry, actor, activist, and cofounder of Inspire Justice**

"*Decolonizing Wealth* offers an arrow to pierce the status quo. It outlines a Native-generated constellation of insights and pathways toward being in right relationship with each other through exploring and amplifying the inherent power and resilience of Native Peoples and ways that the philanthropic sector can heal, learn, and grow—and ultimately can serve individual and collective liberation from centuries of oppression."

—Tia Oros Peters (Shiwi), Executive Director, Seventh Generation Fund for Indigenous Peoples

"*Decolonizing Wealth* is a transformative love letter to humanity. As Edgar says, all of our suffering is mutual and all of our healing is mutual. If we are to have true belonging and justice in our lives and public spaces, then we all must heal—and this book provides a wisdom-led guide on how that can be achieved."

—Dawn-Lyen Gardner, actor, activist, and founder of Belong

"Edgar has challenged the status quo and held a mirror up to the white supremacist philanthropic structures and constructs that perpetuate inequity in society today while offering a hand of healing and justice. This book and Edgar's leadership are very important for this nation as we head into an era of repair that has the potential to build a pathway forward for true transformation and equity."

—Nick Tilsen (Oglala Lakota), President and CEO, NDN Collective

"By anchoring the solutions to America's ills in the wisdom and knowledge of its original people, Edgar challenges all of us working in the nonprofit and philanthropy sectors to analyze how our nation's history of racism and disenfranchisement has infected its financial and giving institutions. I strongly recommend this book as a key resource for funders and advocates to ensure their investments are truly equitable and benefiting the lives of people and communities of color."

—Heather McGhee, author, political commentator, and former President, Demos

"We are all on a journey of self-reckoning—every CEO, every executive, everyone. With his vital and timely book, *Decolonizing Wealth*, Edgar provides a means of having those necessary conversations, including with yourself. We all have the opportunity to progress, and this book provides an important pathway for that."

—David Linde, CEO, Participant

DECOLONIZING WEALTH

DECOLONIZING WEALTH

Indigenous Wisdom to Heal Divides and Restore Balance

Second Edition

Edgar Villanueva

Foreword by Bishop William J. Barber II

BK®

Berrett–Koehler Publishers, Inc.

Berrett-Koehler Publishers, Inc.
1333 Broadway, Suite 1000
Oakland, CA 94612-1921
Tel: (510) 817-2277; Fax: (510) 817-2278
www.bkconnection.com

ORDERING INFORMATION
Quantity sales. Special discounts are available on quantity purchases by corporations, associations, and others. For details, contact the "Special Sales Department" at the Berrett-Koehler address above.
Individual sales. Berrett-Koehler publications are available through most bookstores. They can also be ordered directly from Berrett-Koehler: Tel: (800) 929-2929; Fax: (802) 864-7626; www.bkconnection.com.
Orders for college textbook / course adoption use. Please contact Berrett-Koehler: Tel: (800) 929-2929; Fax: (802) 864-7626.

Distributed to the U.S. trade and internationally by Penguin Random House Publisher Services.

Berrett-Koehler and the BK logo are registered trademarks of Berrett-Koehler Publishers, Inc.

Printed in Canada

Berrett-Koehler books are printed on long-lasting acid-free paper. When it is available, we choose paper that has been manufactured by environmentally responsible processes. These may include using trees grown in sustainable forests, incorporating recycled paper, minimizing chlorine in bleaching, or recycling the energy produced at the paper mill.

Library of Congress Cataloging-in-Publication Data
Names: Villanueva, Edgar, author. | Barber, William J., II, 1963-, writer of foreword.
Title: Decolonizing wealth : indigenous wisdom to heal divides and restore balance / Edgar Villanueva ; foreword by Bishop William J. Barber II.
Description: Second edition. | Oakland, CA : Berrett-Koehler Publishers, [2021] | Includes bibliographical references and index.
Identifiers: LCCN 2021016165 | ISBN 9781523091416 (paperback) | ISBN 9781523091423 (adobe pdf) | ISBN 9781523091430 (epub)
Subjects: LCSH: Income distribution--United States. | Wealth--United States. | Unjust enrichment--United States. | Restitution--United States. | Indians of North America--United States. | Slavery--United States. | Postcolonialism--United States.
Classification: LCC HC110.I5 V55 2021 | DDC 339.2/20973--dc23
LC record available at https://lccn.loc.gov/2021016165

Second Edition
27 26 25 24 23   10 9 8 7 6 5 4 3 2

Cover design: Idea2Form and Irene Morris
Front cover author photo: Adam Ouahmane
Interior design: Mayapriya Long, Bookwrights
Book production: Seventeenth Street Studios

To the memory of my grandmother, Gracie Bryant Miller (1936–2020), our unassuming matriarch and resident comedian. We miss you. To my mother, Sheila Jacobs, her caretaker and the first philanthropist I knew. I love you.

"If we are going to heal, let it be glorious."
—Beyoncé

Contents

Foreword

This book is a call to repair society's breaches by re-allocating resources to heal our divisions and address inequality in our society. In the ancient biblical text, the prophet Isaiah tells us that if you "spend yourselves on behalf of the hungry and satisfy the needs of the oppressed," then "your people will rebuild the ancient ruins and raise up the age-old foundations" (Isaiah 58). Reconstructing a just and merciful society is possible, but it depends upon a commitment to invest in repairing age-old harms.

Brother Edgar Villanueva has internalized the prophet's wisdom and is inviting us to practice it today. The path to healing that he offers in these pages is welcoming to all, and it is a path that can unite people from all walks of life, from people in our streets to the people in this nation's suites. This moment in our nation is not about left, right, or centrist. It should not be about Republicans and Democrats. This is a moment when the Indigenous principle of "all my relations" can rise like a beacon and light the road to repair and healing.

Edgar has emerged from the institutions of philanthropy, which like all powerful institutions are full of false prophets who wield altruism as a kind of smoke and mirrors, obscuring the sources of their wealth. America's wealth was made off of stolen lands and on the backs of enslaved and poor workers. Those who "give away" money to feed the poor with one hand while continuing to create conditions that keep people poor with the other are not repairing the breach but perpetuating it. This book tears away any illusions about that being the way. We must insist on the wealthy paying their fair share of taxes, for only then can we afford to ensure universal health care, living wages, fully funded public education, affordable housing, and a robust program to address the climate crisis.

People in power have refused to see poverty for too long. The first thing we have to do is demand that America see her poverty. It's a fundamental moral principle of this democracy that everybody has a right to live with dignity. When we relaunched the Poor People's Campaign in 2018—the same year that the first edition of this book appeared—it was to continue the work that Dr. Martin Luther King Jr. and so many others had begun 50 years prior, in 1968. Somebody in every age has to challenge this country to be true to its moral foundation in the Constitution, the Declaration of Independence, and our deepest religious values. This is a call as old as the ancient prophet's. But it is our time now.

Edgar's roots are in the community I hold dear. His ancestors are the original inhabitants of the land we know as North Carolina, and his roots include the evangelical Christian tradition that is my own. I recognize in his work and his words the profound influence of the teachings of Jesus, who said "Love your neighbor as yourself."

What does it mean to love our neighbor? It is a question that resonates in the hearts of those of any faith, as well as in the hearts of those of no particular faith who long to live in a healthy and just world. It is a question that is not bounded by the walls of any church. It is a question that must be taken up in the halls of government, on the sets of films and TV shows, in classrooms and the boardrooms of corporations and foundations, across the nation and indeed the world. What conversations, actions, and policies must we implement? It is the question at the heart of this book: How can we truly love our neighbor?

I want to thank Edgar for his contribution to the healing that is needed if we are to rebuild the ancient ruins and repair the breaches of our society. May we invest all of the resources we have at our disposal in the work that is necessary to bring about a Third Reconstruction in America today.

Bishop William J. Barber II
President and Senior Lecturer, Repairers of the Breach
Co-chair, Poor People's Campaign: A National Call for
Moral Revival

INTRODUCTION

What if Money Could Heal Us

This is primarily a book for people who direct the flow of money. The more money you direct, the more this book is for you. You may be a philanthropist, an investor, or a funds manager; you may work for a foundation, a bank, or a community. You may be an "ordinary person" interested in the money invested through your pension or insurance. You may think of yourself as wealthy; maybe you would never use that word. Across the board, according to the numbers, you're more likely to be a white man, since more white men direct more of the flow of money.[1] But you also may be a woman, Black, brown, Indigenous, or anything else that is not a white man.

More broadly, this is also a book for anyone who is interested in healing the wounds of racism, colonization, and dehumanization. This second edition has been expanded to include stories of people working in fields beyond philanthropy and finance, who have been inspired to apply the lessons and Indigenous wisdom from the book to their sector. There's medicine here for you.

1

Whoever you are, you are welcome. As I will explain, in my own Native American belief system, we are all relatives, literally all related to one another. We are also all infected with what I call the "colonizer virus," which urges us to divide, control, and exploit. Nowhere is the virus more symptomatic than in how we deal with wealth.

For some, reading this book may feel like I'm yanking off the Band-Aid. There may be moments of discomfort. I invite you to sit with it, in the understanding that I am motivated by love and that things have been just as uncomfortable, if not really painful, for many of us, for a very long time.

In order to heal what hurts, to come back together as one human race, and to restore balance to the land, we need to decolonize wealth. This book will explain how we can begin to heal ourselves, using money as our medicine.

~~~

$160 million. That's how much money I have given away since 2005. Just under a million per month.

That's a significant sum for all but a handful of extremely wealthy people on the planet. It's even more astonishing given that I grew up in poverty. My people are dirt poor. They hail from Robeson County, North Carolina, the third-poorest county in the United States, where more than a third of folks, including most of my extended family, live on less than $15,000 per year. Yet—unfathomably, from the perspective of my family—I've made close to $160 million in philanthropic gifts. If that were 1.3 percent of my income—which is the average annual percentage given as donations by the super-wealthy[2]—I would have to be earning around $770 million every year.

I would, that is, if that money were my own. As it happens, I am that rare phenomenon: a Native American working in the field of philanthropy. Those millions are other people's money, entrusted to my hands.

~~~~

The field of philanthropy is a living anachronism.

It is (we are) like a stodgy relative wearing clothes that will never come back in fashion. The field is adamant that it knows best, holding tight the purse strings. It is stubborn. It fails to get with the times, frustrating the younger folks. It does not care.

It is (we are) like a mansion with neoclassical columns and manicured lawns, staffed with butlers and maids who pass silver trays of tiny tasteless nibbles (*pigs in blankets, angels on horseback, anyone?*) to guests wearing tailcoats and bustles, as a string quartet plays tunes written centuries ago. No one's voice rises over a certain decibel, no one jokes, no one's words call attention to the ludicrous and unsustainable farce that is the entire scene.

It is (we are) a period play, a costume drama, a fantasy of entitlement, altruism, and superiority. Far too often, it creates (we create) division and suffering rather than progress and healing.

It is (we are) a sleepwalking sector, white zombies spewing the money of dead white people in the name of charity and benevolence.

It is (we are) colonialism in the empire's newest clothes.

It is (we are) racism in institutional form.

Philanthropy moves at a glacial pace. Epidemics and storms hit, communities go under water literally and metaphorically, Black and brown children get shot dead or lose their youth inside jail cells, families are separated across continents, women are abused and beaten and raped, all of Rome burns while we fiddle with another survey on strategies, another study on impact.

Other sectors feel the heat of competition. Not us. We politely nod at the innovations of the business sector; it takes us a half century to implement one of them. We indulge those who say that diversity is important by conducting several decades of analyses, hiring consulting groups with absurd price tags. We publish reports. We create a task force and debate mightily over what to call it. We do not actually change, not more than superficially.

This is philanthropy. It is (we are) the family that embarrasses me and infuriates me. But it's still my family, my relations, and I believe in redemption. It's from the place of calling this family to a better self that I write.

Philanthropy, honey, it's time for an intervention.

~~~

Most critiques of philanthropy point the accusing finger at things like funding priorities, grantmaking decision processes, the tax code, and payout percentages. As far as I'm concerned, a focus on reforming this stuff is certainly valid, but ultimately it is about as effective as rearranging the deck chairs on the *Titanic*. Why? Because those are mere symptoms of a virus that has pervaded every aspect, every cell, every interaction. What remains unexamined with those kinds of reforms are frank conversations about where that wealth came from, why it's held back from public coffers, how it's invested as an endowment, and who gets to manage, allocate, and spend it.

My central argument is that what ails philanthropy at its core is colonialism. Almost without exception, funders reinforce the colonial division of Us versus Them, Haves versus Have-Nots, and mostly white saviors and white experts versus *poor, needy, urban, disadvantaged, marginalized, at-risk* people (take your pick of euphemisms for people of color). The statistics speak for themselves: 90 percent of foundation CEOs are white,[3] 85 percent of foundation boards are white,[4] while no more than 10 percent of foundation funding goes specifically to people of color.[5] Philanthropy is the savior mentality in institutional form, which instead of helping—its ostentatiously proclaimed intent—actually further divides and destabilizes society.

Part 1 of this book, "Where It Hurts," recounts my journey into the heart of philanthropy, past the field's glamorous, altruistic facade, into its shadows. I drill down to the core of the affliction, uncovering white supremacy, the savior mentality, and internalized oppression.

Yet while my own experience is centered in philanthropy, the same dynamics basically hold true across what I call the loans-to-gifts spectrum: Bank loans. Venture capital. Municipal bonds. Even social and ethical finance, impact investments, and humanitarian aid. Here, the statistics are equally dismal. The C-suite of financial services is 90 percent white[6] and 70 percent of venture capitalists are white,[7] as are more than 87 percent of angel investors.[8] On the receiving side, loan requests from Black entrepreneurs are three times more likely to be denied than are requests from white entrepreneurs.[9] In 2020, a measly 2.6 percent of venture capital funding went to African American and Latinx entrepreneurs.[10]

To sum it up: when it comes to getting or giving access to money, white men are usually in charge, and everyone else has to be twice as good (or more) to get half as much (or less). All the institutions along the loans-to-gifts spectrum—I'll use the term "funders" to encompass them all—are "ivory towers," by which I mean institutions of racism and division. All these funders exist to preserve the wealth and privilege of a few, to separate them from the rest of us. Most employ money in the name of division, to reinforce fear, greed, and envy.

Now, some will say that it's "just the economy, stupid," the natural outcome of an ideology that puts the welfare of the free market and the rights of corporations before the welfare and rights of people. But I say that those who would focus the blame on the system of capitalism or neoliberalism are obscuring the real root of the problem. As Malcolm X said, "You can't have capitalism without racism."[11]

Since at least the 1400s, white supremacy has been the justification for colonization, the conquest and exploitation of non-European lands, backed by a claim of divine sanction. European white imperialism spent centuries marching around the world, using whatever means necessary to amass and consolidate resources and wealth. Now, adding insult to injury, those who were stolen from or exploited to make that wealth—Indigenous people, people of African descent, and many other people of color—must apply for access to that wealth in the form of loans or grants; we must prove ourselves worthy. We are demeaned for our lack of resources, scrutinized, and often denied access after all.

The tactics of colonization violate us and leave us traumatized, over generations, to this very day.

Yet there's a silver lining in this cataclysm. All of us who have been forced to the margins are the very ones who harbor the best solutions for healing, progress, and peace, by virtue of our outsider perspectives and resilience. When we reclaim our share of resources, when we recover our places at the table and the drawing board, we can design our healing. We can create new ways of seeking and granting access to money. We can return balance to the world by moving money to where the hurt is worst.

To paraphrase Maya Angelou: once we know better, we need to do better.

Money as Medicine

For most people, *medicine* is something used to treat or cure a disease; it is often a human-made drug, or sometimes an herb. Sometimes it refers to the whole field of medicine: hospitals, pharmacies, doctors, and so on. In Native traditions, however, medicine is a way of achieving balance. An Indigenous medicine person doesn't just heal illnesses—he or she can restore harmony or establish a state of being, such as peacefulness. Medicine people live and practice among the people; access to them is constant and unrestricted. And the practice of medicine is not just limited to the hands of medicine people; everyone is welcome to participate. Engaging with medicine is a part of the experience of daily life. Traditionally, Indigenous people don't wait to be out of balance before they turn to medicine.

In the Indigenous worldview, many kinds of things can be medicine: a place, a word, a stone, an animal, a natural phenomenon, a dream, a life event like a coffee date with a friend, or even something that seems bad in the moment, such as the loss of a job. Have you ever looked back at your life and thought, *That was the best thing that could have ever happened to me*? That was medicine. In order for something or someone to serve as medicine, it only needs to be filled with or granted a kind of mystical or spiritual power. Anyone can find and use medicine, just by allowing intuition and feelings to determine whether something can serve as medicine. You listen for its sacred power; you don't force it.

You don't choose the medicine, the elders say. It chooses you.

In part 2 of this book, "Being a Healer," I describe a number of forms of medicine and how various people were able to recognize the medicine that had chosen them. In particular, there's a kind of medicine to which we all have access: our own story. For me, the medicine that is my story only became clear to me later; what chose me first was money.

It has taken me a long, long time (patience is a virtue in Indian country) to accept that the medicine that chose me is money. Because, I mean, money? Come on. Money corrupts. Money is dirty, even filthy. Money is the root of all evil—doesn't the Bible say that?

But what is money but a way to measure value, to facilitate exchange? And what is exchange but a type of relationship between people? Money is a proxy for the sweat we spent on growing food, sewing clothes, assembling electronics, coding apps, creating entertainment, researching and developing innovations, and so on. It's just a stand-in for the materials used, the services granted, the responsibility shouldered. Money is a tool to reflect the obligations to each other that people develop as they interact. It's "the measure of one's trust in other human beings," as anthropologist David Graeber writes in his comprehensive book, *Debt*.[12]

Materially, it's a bit of nickel, zinc, copper. It's a little linen, mostly cotton, some ink. It's basically Kleenex adorned with dead presidents. Actually, today mostly it's a series of zeros and ones. Bytes, data on screens. Imaginary. Harmless.

And in fact, the Bible doesn't say money's the root of all evil. It says the *love* of money is the root of all evil—in other words, it leads to evil when we let it be more important than life, relationships, and humanity.

I'm not saying there aren't problems with money when it's hoarded, controlled, used to divide people, to oppress and dominate. But that's not the money's fault. Inherently, money is value neutral. Humans have used money wrongfully. We've made money more important than human life. We've allowed it to divide us. That *is* a sin. We forget that we humans made money up out of thin air, as a concept, a tool for a complex society, a placeholder for aspects of human relations. We forget that we gave money its meaning and its power.

Money is like water. Water can be a precious life-giving resource. But what happens when water is dammed, or when a water cannon is fired on protesters in subzero temperatures? Money should be a tool of love, to facilitate relationships, to help us thrive, rather than to hurt and divide us. If it's used for sacred, life-giving, restorative purposes, it can be medicine.

Money, used as medicine, can help us decolonize.

Seven Steps to Healing

In part 3 of this book, "How to Heal," I offer my thoughts on what we need to do to decolonize the institutions and processes around money. Across American history and through the present day, the accumulation of wealth is steeped in trauma. The process of healing from that trauma is central to decolonization. Acknowledging our woundedness is key. This is not just for individuals; institutions can also engage in the Seven Steps to Healing:

1. **Grieve.** We have to stop and feel the hurts we've endured.
2. **Apologize.** We must apologize for the hurts we've caused.
3. **Listen.** We must acknowledge the wisdom of those excluded and exploited by the system, who possess exactly the perspective and wisdom needed to fix it.
4. **Relate.** We need space to share our whole selves with each other and understand we don't have to agree in order to respect each other.
5. **Represent.** We must build whole new decision-making tables, rather than setting token places at the colonial tables as an afterthought.
6. **Invest.** We need to put *all* our money where our values are.
7. **Repair.** We must use money to heal where people are hurting and to stop more hurt from happening.

These steps aren't necessarily linear. Certain steps may need to be revisited, and the entire process may need to be repeated. In this way, it's more of a circular or spiral process. Like any clever virus, the colonizer mindset keeps mutating and adapting, so in order to heal fully, we will need to be vigilant and get booster shots.

This is not a silver bullet solution. There is no quick fix for the complexity of colonization. Decolonization is a process with roles for everyone involved, whether you're rich or poor, funder or recipient, victim or perpetrator. It may not feel like we're moving forward at all, during certain phases of healing. Patience and grit are required.

In fact, as you may have already noticed, I don't really do quick fixes; I tell stories. Hello, I'm a Native American! Storytelling, ideally spiced up with a bit of humor, is how we transmit wisdom. Patience is a virtue in Indian country. A lot of books on wealth and finance offer fast-food-style delivery of sound-bites and easy takeaways. Who are those books written by? More often than not, they are not by people who look like me. When someone other than a mainstream white expert is in charge of delivering value and knowledge, the experience is different. I come from a long line of Native storytellers and Southern storytellers. Listening to our stories is part of the decolonization process.

In creating this book, I had the honor and the pleasure of collecting stories from dozens of leaders from foundations, community organizations, and corporations, including financial institutions. Most of them were Indigenous people and people of color; a handful were white folks. I asked them to speak candidly about the dynamics of race and power that they encounter in their work with money, and I asked them to share ideas for how we could decolonize wealth. Because their frank honesty could cause problems for them in their workplace, many chose to be quoted anonymously. I am incredibly grateful for those conversations, which deepened my analysis and furthered my thinking about the relationship between wealth and trauma.

The Lakota say *Mitakuye Oyasin* ("all my relations"), meaning we are all related, connected, not only to each other but also to all the other living things, the inanimate things, the planet, and the Creator. The principle of All My Relations means that everyone is at home here. Everyone has a responsibility for making things right. Everyone has a role in the process of healing, regardless of whether they caused or received more harm. All our suffering is mutual. All our healing is mutual. All our thriving is mutual.

PART ONE

Where It Hurts

I t is true that the first part of this book consists of mostly dark, painful stories, stories of what people endure to gain access to money, stories of the twisted things people do once they have access to money and the power it confers. My own journey through the world of philanthropy forms the backbone, leading to observations about wealth, the colonizer virus, and trauma. Some may say it's tiresome to dwell on the hurt—after all, there's a relentless (if artificial) drive to "Stay positive!" in America, to focus only on solutions. Yet an essential step in the process of decolonization is hearing out the painful stories of the colonized and the exploited, respectfully and with an open heart.

~~~

The chapters in part 1 are named for elements in a slave plantation. As token people of color working within the field of philanthropy, one of our regular watercooler conversations over the years, held in hushed voices, revolves around the analogy of a plantation. Those seeking funding are the people with the least power—the field hands, begging for scraps, given no dignity and treated with no respect. One step up, people of color working in philanthropy, are the house slaves, because we get to be close to the power and the privilege. We benefit from our position in all kinds of ways. Different enslaved people behave differently once they get inside the master's house. Some help those who are still out in the fields. But others take on the characteristics of the master and lord it over those less fortunate. They do whatever it takes to keep their own lucky position intact and unthreatened. Then there are the overseers, usually a white man, but occasionally an enslaved person promoted to the position. Granted, they are in a tough position, under pressure from the master to squeeze as much profit from the slaves as possible, but they are infamous for indifference, delusions of grandeur, and, at worst, cruelty. The overseer in a foundation might be its CEO or executive director.

The plantation metaphor implicitly raises the question of the "master's tools," a reference to the poet and civil rights activist Audre Lorde's declaration, "The master's tools will never dismantle the master's house."[1] In other words, given the level of trauma caused by the colonizer virus and wealth consolidation, can funders actually support transformational change? The master's tools, as I view them, are not money; the tools are anything corrupted to serve the aims of exploitation and domination. If money is an inherently neutral force, as I described in the introduction, then it can also be used for good, as medicine, as I will explore in part 2.

~~~

There is a folktale about a serpent that once upon a time was plaguing a village. The serpent had devoured many of the villagers, including children, and everyone lived in fear of its next attack. A flute player who was still among the living decided something must be done. He packed a bundle of food and a knife, and he went to the edge of the village and began playing his flute. As he expected, the music drew the serpent to him, and in one bite the serpent swallowed the flute player. It was dark inside the serpent's stomach, but the flute player pulled out his knife and cut away a little of the serpent's stomach and ate it. Bit by bit, he cut away the serpent's flesh from the inside. This went on for some time, until finally the flute player reached the serpent's heart. When he cut it out, the serpent died, and the flute player crawled out of the serpent and returned to the village, bringing along the serpent's heart to show everyone, so they would know they no longer had reason to be afraid.

I see this as a story about grappling with collective trauma. We have to enter into the darkness of it. It can't be dealt with from the outside. We have to go inside, despite our resistance, and allow ourselves to feel swallowed up and surrounded by it. It might seem like the pain will never end and there is no way out of it, but bit by bit we come to the heart of the matter. The flute player had prepared himself for a prolonged reckoning. Some kinds of grappling, for especially deep wounds, are lifelong projects. If we do not reckon with it, however, if we carry around unresolved grief, we will spend our lives plagued by the serpent. When we finally get to the heart of the matter, we can emerge lighter and ready to build something new.

CHAPTER ONE

Stolen and Sold

How notions of separation and race resulted in colonization and trauma

Who's *your people?* That's the first question Lumbee Indians ask when we meet someone new, as if we're working out a massive imaginary family tree for humanity in our heads and need to place you on the appropriate limb, branch, or twig. We even sell a T-shirt that has that printed on it: "Who's your people?"

I throw people off with my Latino-sounding last name, which came from my nonbiological father, who was in fact Filipino. He was in my mom's life, and therefore in my life, for a brief moment between the ages of zero and two. When I'm with other Lumbees, I have to mention the last names of my grandfather and grandmother, Jacobs and Bryant, so they know where to place me in the Lumbee family tree. A Lumbee will keep an ear out for our most common surnames, like Brooks, Chavis, Lowry, Locklear. As soon as you say you're related to these families, the stories unfold: *I knew your great-grandfather. I knew your auntie.* There's always a connection.

If you've never met a Native American in person before, you might be saddled with some common misconceptions about me. I have never lived in a teepee. I've never even lived on a reservation. I can't survive in the wilderness on my own. I can't kill or skin a deer. Shoot, I can't even build a fire. No, I didn't get a free education (still paying off those loans!), and yes, I pay taxes.

It wasn't until my late twenties that I really began the process of deeply connecting with my Native heritage. There were three main reasons for this: One, I'm an urban Indian. At least half to three-quarters of us are. Note, "urban" doesn't necessarily mean we live in cities; it's a term that refers to all Indians who do not live on reservations. And yes, I use the terms "Native American" and "(American) Indian" interchangeably. Unless you're an Indian too, you're probably better off sticking with "Native American," just to keep things simple.

Two: I've spent the majority of my adult life working in philanthropy, basically the whitest, most elite sector ever.

Three: I'm Lumbee.

The people known today as Lumbee are the survivors of several tribes who lived along the coast of what is now North Carolina. Those ancestors were the first point of contact for the Europeans, in the late 1500s. So we have had nearly 500 years of interaction with the settlers. Contrast this with some of the West Coast tribes, for many of whom the experience of colonization has been going on for just 200-some years, less than half the time. My people have been penetrated by and exposed to whiteness for a long, long time—longer than any other North American Native community. We assimilated to survive. The fact that any shred of anything remotely appearing to be Native exists among us is really a miracle. "Resilience" has become a trendy word in conversations about business, insurance, and climate. Let me tell you, my people really have a corner on resilience.

Originally Sioux-, Algonquin-, and Iroquois-speaking people, today Lumbees have no language to call our own, although we have a distinctive dialect on top of the southern North Carolina accent. We have so fully embraced Christianity that when you go to apply for or renew your tribal membership card, you are asked which church you attend. While we maintain our notion of tribal sovereignty, we are pretty thoroughly colonized.

There are people who deny that Lumbees are Native at all, as if a group of opportunists just came together to make this tribe up because they wanted to get some government money. Honestly, that's ridiculous. All you have to do is go to Robeson County, North Carolina, where there are 60,000 people concentrated who definitely are not quite white or Black. Some of them look as stereotypically Indian as Sitting Bull, as my maternal grandfather did. Lumbee physical characteristics are on a spectrum from presenting white to presenting Black, because the area historically has been a third, a third, a third—Lumbee, Black, and white—and there has been some intermingling over the last half millennium. In fact, the most probable fate of the famous Lost Colony of Roanoke—the group of English settlers led by Sir Walter Raleigh who arrived in 1584—is that they didn't disappear at all. They just got hungry and needed help, and the Native coastal Indians, my ancestors, took them in and integrated them. There have been linguistic studies on the British influences within the Lumbee dialect that further support that theory.[1]

Other Native tribes give Lumbees a hard time because of anti-Black racism. Indians elsewhere in the country have said things to me like, "Oh, you guys are not really Indian. You play hip-hop at your powwows" (which is not true!). Or they've said we're not Indian because we're not fully recognized by the federal government. There's such a scarcity mentality—part of the legacy of the colonizers' competitive mindset—that there are Indians who fear there will be fewer federal resources paid out to them if more unrecognized Indians receive federal recognition.

It was only in 1956 that the U.S. Congress recognized Lumbees as Indians by passing the Lumbee Act, but the full benefits of federal recognition were not ensured in the act, and to this day we are still fighting for the federal legislation that would do so. In 2020, legislation that would grant Lumbees full federal recognition passed the House of Representatives but failed to receive approval from the Senate.[2] There are eight tribes in North Carolina, and only one, the Eastern Band of the Cherokee Nation, is federally recognized. Any of us could be unrecognized tomorrow. Federal recognition is given and taken away by the stroke of a pen. There have been tribes who were granted federal recognition by one administration, until the next president who came in took it away—this happened to the Duwamish Tribe in Seattle.[3] We're all subject to someone who is not an Indian himself (it's usually a him) calling those shots.

When I was a child growing up in Raleigh, North Carolina, in the 1980s, official forms had boxes for "White," "Black," and "Other." Until the migration of Latinos into the state in the 1990s, and later the Asians who came when Research Triangle Park really took off, Natives were usually the only people in the Other box. I always had to check the Other box. For the most part, that was the extent of my Native identity, because no one was stirring up Native pride or celebrating Lumbee heritage in my school. My family was more focused on survival.

Being Native American inherently involves an identity crisis. We're the only race or ethnicity that is only acknowledged if the government says we are. Here we are, we exist, but we still have to prove it. Anyone else can say they are what they are. No one has to prove that they're Black or prove that they're Latino. There are deep implications to this. The rates of alcoholism, substance abuse, and suicide are linked to this fundamental questioning of our identity. We exist in the Other box. To try to feel safe inside that box, and then be told you've got to prove your right to be in that box, that the box itself is under threat, is deeply demoralizing.

My identity as a Native American is complicated. It's been a long journey to decolonize myself and connect more deeply with my Indigenous heritage. Still, it's the bedrock foundation of my identity. If I were a tree, my Native identity would be my core, the very first ring.

Unpacking Colonization

Colonization seems totally normal because the history books are full of it—and because to this day many colonizing powers talk about colonization not with shame but with pride in their accomplishments. It's so strange. Conquering is one thing: you travel to another place and take its resources, kill the people who get in your way, and then go home with your spoils. But in colonization, you stick around, occupy the land, and force the existing Indigenous people to *become you*. It's like a zombie invasion; colonizers insist on taking over the bodies, minds, and souls of the colonized.

Who came up with this, and why?

Without going too deep into the details of humanity's evolution (there are other great books for that),[4] I just say that the concept of colonization followed the trend that seems to have begun when humans first became farmers and began managing, controlling, and "owning" other forms of life—plant and animal (giving us this horrifying word, "livestock"). Conceptually, this required that humans think of themselves as separate from the rest of the natural world.

This was the beginning of a divergence from the Indigenous worldview, which fundamentally seeks not to own or control but to coexist with and steward the land and nonhuman forms of life. As the philosopher Derek Rasmussen put it, "What makes a people Indigenous? Indigenous people believe they belong to the land, and non-Indigenous people believe the land belongs to them."[5] It's not that Indigenous people were or are without strife or violence, but their fundamental worldview emphasizes connection, reciprocity, a circular dynamic.

It's important to remember that a worldview is a human creation. It's not our destiny. It's not inevitable. Even though it came close to disappearing entirely as the separation worldview took hold and became dominant over several centuries, the Indigenous worldview persisted.

The separation worldview, on an individual level but also at every level of complexity, goes like this:

> The boundaries of my body separate me from the rest of the universe. I'm on my own against the world. This terrifies me, and so I try to control everything outside myself, also known as the Other. I fear the Other; I must compete with the Other in

order to meet my needs. I always need to act in my
self-interest, and I blame the Other for everything
that goes wrong.

Separation correlates with fear, scarcity, and blame, all
of which arise when we think we're not together in this
thing called life. In the separation worldview, humans are
divided from and set above nature, mind is separated from
and elevated above body, and some humans are considered
distinct from and valued above others—us versus them—
as opposed to seeing ourselves as part of a greater whole.

This fundamentally divisive mindset led to an endless
number of categories by which to further divide up the
world and then rank them, assigning to one side the lower
rank, the lesser power. So the rational took its place and
lorded over the emotional, male over female, expert over
amateur, and so on. In every sector, the very structure and
approach of organizations also reflected a divisive, pigeon-
holing, and ranking mindset.

The separation-based economy exploits natural
resources and most of the planet's inhabitants for the profit
of a few. It considers the earth an object, separate from us,
with its resources existing solely for human use, rather
than understanding the earth as a living biosphere of which
we are just one part. Money, of course, has been used and is
still constantly used to separate people—most fundamentally, into Haves and Have-Nots.

Separation-based political systems create arbitrary
nation-states with imaginary boundaries. Their laws and
institutions oppress some groups and privilege others.
Leaders and experts are considered a special breed, set
apart from the common person; all the important choices
are up to them. The separation-based political conversation

revolves around the questions: *Whom should we fear?* and *Whom should we blame?*

Most damaging of all, a long line of mostly white male bullies and sociopaths took the concept of separation and used it to justify oppression, slavery, and colonization by "scientifically" claiming the inferiority of Africans and Indigenous people, among other Others. And so we got to white supremacy.

~~~

I use the term "white supremacy" instead of "racism" because it explicitly names who in the system benefits and—implicitly—who bears the burden. One of the tactics of domination is to control the language around the perpetrator's bad behavior. To call the phenomenon "racism" makes it abstract and erases explicit mention of the one who profits from the dynamic. So when I say "white supremacy" it doesn't just mean the KKK, the Proud Boys, and other hate groups.

White supremacy is a bizarre mythology created by people with pale skin. It asserts that paler people deserve more—more respect, more resources, more opportunity—for no reason beyond the utterly arbitrary and ultimately meaningless pigmentation of their skin. It says that pale people make the important decisions while people of color pay the price. Pale people define what is normal; they make the rules. Whiteness is the default, the standard, the norm; when it goes without saying what someone's ethnic background is, it's because they are pale. Pale people fill the airwaves, screens, and history books with their stories, until it is hard to find heroes and role models who are not pale.

"This system rests on the historical and current accumulation of structural power that privileges, centralizes, and elevates white people as a group," writes Robin DiAngelo, the whiteness studies professor who also coined the term "white fragility," which refers to the discomfort and resistance white people often express when these issues are raised. Fragile or not, the not just historical but also present-day evidence is hard to dispute. DiAngelo again:

If, for example, we look at the racial breakdown of the people who control our institutions, we see that in 2016–2017:

Congress: 90 percent white

Governors: 96 percent white

Top military advisors: 100 percent white

President and vice president: 100 percent white

Current U.S. presidential cabinet: 91 percent white

People who decide which TV shows we see: 93 percent white

People who decide which books we read: 90 percent white

People who decide which news is covered: 85 percent white

People who decide which music is produced: 95 percent white

Teachers: 83 percent white

Full-time college professors: 84 percent white[6]

Despite welcome and desperately needed shifts in some of these statistics since 2018—for example, 2019's Congress was 22 percent people of color, bringing it down to 78 percent white—and, as of 2021, we have a woman of color vice president and a more diverse cabinet—the fact remains that the numbers continue to be skewed toward whiteness. Given that white people currently constitute only 60 percent of American citizens, you can see how far out of proportion those statistics are. Since the Trump election, the "whitelash" (per CNN commentator Van Jones) that followed our first Black president, and the resurrection of emboldened racism across the country, many of us feel this imbalance is only going to get worse.

Vanessa Daniel, executive director of the Groundswell Fund, calls the dynamic "the hubris of white supremacist conquest and imperialism and its insatiable thirst for total dominance over nature, over people of color, over anyone who is not white, Christian, cisgender, male, and rich. It has been a termite-like force that throughout history has eviscerated all in its path."[7]

Only recently has white supremacy begun to be called out. Its invisibility and taken-for-grantedness has been part of its enduring power. "If we can't identify it, we can't interrupt it," says DiAngelo.[8] In a world of white supremacy, white people are considered credible, the experts and authorities, while nonwhite people are often dismissed as untrustworthy and unreliable. When, over decades, the police, courts, banks, schools, and other parts of society regularly ignore, exploit, and harm nonwhite people, yet these incidents are largely denied, excused, or blamed on the victims, without being properly investigated, before disappearing from the accounts of history or the evening news or the general discourse—this is white supremacy. The humanity of certain people is made invisible.

At its height in the early 1920s (not very long ago!), the British Empire governed close to a fifth of the world's population and a quarter of the world's total land.[9] When a 2014 poll among British citizens finds that 59 percent feel that their colonial activities are a source of pride, outnumbering those who feel colonization was a source of shame by three to one, that is white supremacy. When half of those polled state they believe the countries that were colonized were better off for being colonized, that's white supremacy, alive and kicking, in the twenty-first century.[10]

The widespread ambivalence today among the citizens of colonizing powers about whether or not colonization was a good thing is deeply offensive. Make no mistake: colonization is an atrocity, a close relative of genocide.

Divide, Control, Exploit

As far back as the 1400s, white supremacy, often in the name of Christianity, was employed to justify colonization—the conquest and exploitation of non-European lands—by claiming the inferiority of Africans and Indigenous people. The Christian Doctrine of Discovery specified that the entire world was under the jurisdiction of the pope, as God's representative on earth. Any land not under the sovereignty of a Christian ruler could be possessed on behalf of God. European colonizers sailed around the world, taking stuff that didn't belong to them and asserting that it was their God-given right to do so.

Academics who study colonization distinguish between external or exploitation colonization—in which the focus is on extracting goods like tea, silk, or sugar, or resources like human labor, coltan, or oil, in order to increase the wealth and power of the colonizer—and internal colonization, which seeks to manage and control people inside the borders of the empire, using tools like schooling, policing, segregation, surveillance, and divestment. These two kinds of colonialism can and often do coexist. Violence and exploitation are always part of the process. The mantra of colonizers is "Divide, control, [and above all] exploit."

In many countries around the world, the colonizers came, wreaked their havoc, and at some point left, sometimes after uprisings and independence movements succeeded in pushing them out. In America, however, they stayed. This is known as settler colonialism. Manifest Destiny, the rallying cry for westward expansion of the United States, was the Doctrine of Discovery updated for the nineteenth century.

In order to lay claim to land that did not belong to them, settlers had to erase everyone and everything that came before. They rewrote history to legitimize their actions. They had to find a way to justify their atrocious behavior, by claiming to be more deserving, more civilized, and superior to the original inhabitants, the First Nations. The settlers claimed their god granted them the right. And to be clear: *settlers cannot be considered immigrants* because immigrants are expected to obey the laws of the land when they arrive, while settlers make their own new laws of the land.

In all scenarios, colonization has deep, long-lasting impacts on the colonized, the natives, but settler colonialism makes things much, much messier. The Tunisian author Albert Memmi wrote, "It is not easy to escape mentally from a concrete situation, to refuse its ideology *while continuing to live with its actual relationships.*"[11] What makes it even more complicated in the United States is that, over time, the white settlers brought slaves and later attracted low-wage workers—many of them people of color—who all were hurt and exploited and yet also were technically settlers, from the Indigenous perspective.

The settlers caused death, disease, diaspora, and cultural subjugation of Native communities. They systematically suppressed our Native governance and sovereignty. They systematically delegitimized and stamped out our traditional, holistic ways of understanding, learning, and knowing. Forced removals traumatized Natives by severing us from the lands that contained the plants and animals we needed to sustain the physical, mental, cultural, and spiritual health of our communities. Our lands also contained the bones of our ancestors and the keys to our traditional ways of life. When all these efforts and policies failed to extinguish us, the settlers launched the era of "boarding schools," separating Native children from their families and cultures, cutting off our hair, forbidding us to speak our languages, forcing us to act white. *Divide, control, exploit.*

Honestly, it's amazing that we survived at all.

These atrocities took place over hundreds of years, depending on where the Native community was located. Remember that my people were the first point of contact for the Europeans in the late 1500s and thus have nearly 500 years of experience with the settlers, whereas for the Natives of California, the experience of colonization has been going on for just about 200 years. This means that for many California Indians, the traumas experienced by their ancestors remain quite alive in community memory. At every gathering of Natives I attend, there are elders who as children experienced being ripped away from their families and homes and being forced to submit to indoctrination in white boarding schools. The horrors are that fresh.

~~~

Beginning in the 1960s, an era of Indigenous activism and tribal self-determination led to major reforms in policies directed at Native nations and Indigenous people in the United States, which coincided with the civil rights movement. The reforms included the Indian Child Welfare Act, the Native American Graves Protection and Repatriation Act, the American Indian Religious Freedom Act, and the Indian Self-Determination and Education Assistance Act—all of which provided much clearer federal acknowledgment of, and support for, tribal sovereignty, as well as self-determination in policies affecting our health, safety, and well-being. On the international level, the United Nations finally raised the issue of Indigenous rights in the 1990s, and in 2000 they established the United Nations Permanent Forum on Indigenous Issues.

Nevertheless, despite these events, Natives everywhere still face considerable challenges. In the United States today, there are 2.9 million Natives, or 0.9 percent of the population, and 5.2 million Natives mixed with other races, or 1.7 percent of the population.[12] At 11 percent, our unemployment rate is almost double the national rate of 6.2 percent, while our median incomes are a third lower than the national average.[13] Our high school dropout rates are nearly twice as high as the national average,[14] while our youth are three and a half times more likely to commit suicide.[15] According to U.S. Department of Justice records, one in three Native American women is raped in their lifetime, a figure that is two and a half times greater than the average for all U.S. women. In 86 percent of cases of rape of Indigenous women and girls, the rapist is non-Native, which results in many crimes going uninvestigated by either U.S. or tribal officials, because the jurisdiction is unclear.[16] While Native American youth only make up 1.8 percent of the total youth population, they represent 3.6 percent of those detained, and once they are in the prison system, they are more likely to be placed in detention and less likely to get probation.[17] During the COVID-19 pandemic, as of December 2020, the mortality rate was twice as high for Native Americans as for white folks.[18] In addition to loss of life, tribes lost an estimated $4.4 billion in economic activity and $997 million in wages during the pandemic,[19] which exacerbates existing economic disparities facing Native Americans.

Natives face special health challenges and disparities, too, from having the highest rates of diabetes, heart disease, and asthma among any racial/ethnic group to experiencing persistent barriers to health care and insurance. Tuberculosis, mental illness, major cardiovascular diseases, pneumonia, cancer, infant mortality, and maternal complications are other issues that disproportionately impact Natives.[20]

Urban Indians—those of us who live somewhere other than on reservations—face unique challenges. Federal funding does not always directly address our needs, and the safety net available to Natives living on reservations or tribal territories is unavailable to most of us. The magnitude of this problem is significant, as urban Indians make up more than 70 percent of the Native population overall.[21]

So, although Native American people who are alive today are proud, strong survivors against all odds, we continue to face some of the most dire socioeconomic conditions of any group in America. There is no question that the complicated set of issues facing us today is rooted in hundreds of years of colonization, suffering, and trauma.

Trauma

If you have personally experienced a traumatic event, such as a great loss, a violation, or abuse, you know how it destroys your trust, your sense of safety, even your sense of who you are. In order to survive trauma, you react unconsciously to protect yourself, usually using an automatic survival strategy like dissociation, fight, flight, or appeasing. Often these self-protection and defense mechanisms stick with you, coloring your perception of everyone you meet and everything that happens from then on, especially if you are traumatized more than once. After a while, you have less and less choice in the matter; the protective stance hardens into a way of seeing and experiencing the world. It feels like the way you are: *I'm just distant. I'm just unemotional. I'm just suspicious. I'm just small and unthreatening. I'm just mean and aggressive.* You have blinders on about what is possible for yourself and for human interactions, and you don't even know how much they limit the possibilities.

Unfortunately, almost every one of us alive on earth has experienced some kind of trauma. So chances are you know what I am talking about. But now imagine if you came from generations of people who were systematically and repeatedly violated in every possible way. Imagine that all your family and friends and community members regularly experienced traumatic events—upheaval, violence, rape, brainwashing, homelessness, forced marches, criminalization, denigration, and murder—over hundreds of years. Imagine the trauma of this experience has been reinforced by government policies, economic systems, and social norms that have systematically denied your people access to safety, mobility, resources, food, education, dignity, and positive reflections of themselves. Repeated and ongoing violation, exploitation, and deprivation have a deep, lasting traumatic impact, not just at the individual level but on whole populations, tribes, and nations. This is what's known as collective trauma, historic trauma, intergenerational trauma.

The relatively new field of epigenetics studies how trauma that our ancestors experienced can literally be passed down, attached to our DNA. An essay in a 2013 issue of *Discover* magazine described it this way: "Like silt deposited on the cogs of a finely tuned machine after the seawater of a tsunami recedes, our experiences, and those of our forebears, are never gone, even if they have been forgotten. They become a part of us, a molecular residue holding fast to our genetic scaffolding."[22] It was found, for example, that the descendants of Holocaust survivors had different cortisone profiles than normal, which was an adaptation to prolonged starvation, since cortisol impacts the ability of certain organs to use glucose and metabolic fuels.

My central metaphor for the subject of colonization is the body, because we each instinctively understand our body's sense of sovereignty and the sense of violation. The initial phase of colonization—the conquest—is like a rape, causing the first wave of trauma. Later—when the colonizers set down roots and become settlers—colonization becomes more like a virus that every human institution and system, as well as every human being, carries inside. The collective body—the nation and culture of settlers and surviving colonized people—adapts, passing down these adaptations in their genes over generations. Yet the adaptations don't constitute healing. The virus remains, the original seeds of separation—fear of the Other—that lead to ongoing acts of control and exploitation.

The colonizer virus inside culture and institutions is especially dangerous. Our education system reflects the colonizer virus. So does our agriculture and food system. So does our foreign policy. So does our environmental policy. So does the entertainment industry and the field of design. And so do the realms of wealth, the subject of this book: investment, finance, and philanthropy.

Decolonization

Decolonization, obviously, is the process of undoing colonization. The Afro-Caribbean philosopher and revolutionary Frantz Fanon described decolonization using a famous line from the Bible: "The last shall be first and the first last."[23] Taken literally, decolonization means that the land that was stolen is returned and that sovereignty over not only the land and its resources but also social structures and traditions is granted back to those from whom it was all stolen.

Yet decolonization defined like this tends to get stuck and make no headway at all. The truth is there is no future that does not include the settlers occupying Indigenous lands. Today, in the twenty-first century, Indigenous and settler lives, families, and businesses are intertwined. This is simply the pragmatic reality of today's world. What we *can* focus on with decolonization is stopping the cycles of abuse and healing ourselves from trauma. In this way, we expand our possibilities for the future.

We must heal ourselves by each taking responsibility for our part in creating or maintaining the colonial virus. We must identify and reject the colonized aspects of our culture and our institutions so that we can heal. In healing, we eradicate the colonizer virus from society. Instead of *divide, control, exploit*, we embrace a new paradigm of *connect, relate, belong*.

COLONIZED ⟶ DECOLONIZED

DIVIDE ⟶ CONNECT

CONTROL ⟶ RELATE

EXPLOIT ⟶ BELONG

It seems that the idea of decolonizing is hitting many sectors now. The global response to the murder of George Floyd in 2020 led to a surge of actions challenging and even tearing down monuments and statues to colonizers like King Leopold of Belgium.[24] A December 2020 search on Google for the term "decolonizing" yielded nearly 3 million results, while "decolonization" yielded more than 13 million, with many of the news stories dating from 2018 to 2020. There's a decolonized cookbook. There are decolonized curricula being developed for schools. *Teen Vogue* ran a story in February 2018, "Indigenous Land Acknowledgement, Explained."[25] There's a game called Cards Against Colonization, a play on Cards Against Humanity. A doctor in San Francisco is partnering with Native health care providers to define what decolonized health care looks like. She is already teaching it to medical students. Two researchers out of Stanford are investigating how the colonial mentality influenced organizational design and are proposing tools for decolonizing organizational processes.

My contribution is to address the sectors of banking, investment, finance, philanthropy, and all their institutions and processes and to offer a path to healing. They—we—are all deeply infected with the colonizer virus. Wealth is used to divide us and control us and exploit us, but it doesn't have to be.

CHAPTER TWO

Arriving at the Plantation

How the design, architecture, and location of financial institutions reflect and maintain colonization

In 2005, I was finishing my master's in health care administration at the University of North Carolina at Chapel Hill. Most of my friends in the program were going into hospital administration—it's what our degree was focused on, and there's big money to make in running hospitals. I had interviewed at a few of them, like the Mayo Clinic, but I just didn't feel right about it. All they really wanted to know was if I could figure out how to save them money; healing and helping people was not the first order of business at all. I interviewed at the consulting firm Deloitte, too. None of these jobs felt like ministry, like medicine, like truly being of service. My professor told me there was an opportunity at a foundation called the Kate B. Reynolds Charitable Trust (KBR) and that they were interested in talking to me.

"I think you should go," he said.

Frankly, that didn't sound appealing either. For starters, I was not interested in living in Winston-Salem. It might be North Carolina's fourth-largest city, but that isn't saying much. I had my sights set on a *real* city, which at the time meant DC or Atlanta for this country boy. Still, I dutifully drove to the foundation for my first interview. My old Honda Civic rolled onto the idyllic property—acres of manicured lawns and gardens, a main house with 22 windows flanking the front, a chapel, and a greenhouse. The property even had a name, Reynolda. I had never been to a house with a name. What kind of person names his house?

Reynolda was built by R. J. Reynolds, the tobacco tycoon. When I picture R.J., I think of the Great Gatsby as played by Leonardo DiCaprio: charming and gregarious but also entitled and clueless. R.J.'s father had been a large-scale land and slave owner, a merchant, and a tobacco farmer. By 1860, when R.J. was 10 years old, his father owned two dozen properties, more than 10,000 acres. His 59 slaves made him one of the largest slaveholders in Virginia. After the Civil War, R.J. and his siblings had to help their father adapt to a world without slave labor. African Americans—now freedmen—were still critical to the tobacco business—now as sharecroppers and tenant farmers.

In 1874, R.J. sold his shares in the family business and started his own tobacco company in Winston with his younger brother William Neal. Things really took off for them after they invented prepackaged cigarettes. Long the county's most eligible bachelor, R.J. finally settled down, got hitched, and built the 1,000-plus-acre estate Reynolda, basically a self-contained village for Reynolds employees and their families.

During his lifetime, R.J. supported many charities: schools, churches, orphanages, and hospitals. When he passed away in 1917, he was the wealthiest person in the state by a wide margin. His wife and his children continued his philanthropy, forming several foundations with the family money. The Reynolds name is on buildings everywhere in these parts. Kate B., for whom the Kate B. Reynolds Charitable Trust is named, was the wife of R.J.'s younger brother and business partner, William Neal Reynolds.[1]

In other words, this was quintessential "old money," the inherited wealth of established upper-class families, sometimes called "gentry," or the "de facto aristocracy" because the United States isn't supposed to have an actual aristocratic class. On top of the colonial culture that goes with old money, the Trust also reflected the culture of banking.

In 1947, the Trust was created with just under $5 million from Mrs. Reynolds's estate put in trust at Wachovia Bank, her personal bank. By 1988, assets totaled $129 million. A year later, a New York investment banking firm successfully completed a leveraged buyout of RJR Nabisco, including R.J. Reynolds Tobacco Company, and the Trust received $100 per share of its 2.4 million shares. Literally overnight, Trust assets doubled (several folks in Winston-Salem became instant millionaires), and the Trust began to review opportunities to reduce its initial tax liability by channeling some of the gain to qualified charitable organizations. It also decided to move the staffing structure outside the bank, given the drastic increase in assets. Since then, from its more than 2 million shares of R.J. Reynolds company stock, the Trust has grown to more than $530 million in assets and uses three-fourths of the investment income collected each year to improve the health of low-income people across the state, and the other fourth "to help the poor and needy" in Winston-Salem.

The irony that wealth made from cigarettes is being used to improve health is mostly lost on the community, eager to get a piece of the pie.

Because KBR was literally born and operated from a bank, banking culture prevailed. For most of its history, the leadership of the foundation had been drawn from within Wachovia or was staffed by employees who left the bank to run the external operations. The first president was at Wachovia for 28 years before joining the foundation. He started out in the traditional role of a bank trust officer. He joined the foundation two years after the RJR Nabisco buyout. He maintained a relatively formal, impersonal culture, including strict business attire. Men wore white dress shirts, neckties, and wingtip shoes. The foundation office—specifically built to resemble the original buildings on the Reynolda property, I later learned—had white walls, and all the furniture was heavy, wooden, and antique. It felt like a different time period inside the office.

It was my first experience of how anachronistic the field of philanthropy is, how formal, how distanced from ordinary people's lives and experiences. The atmosphere that compels you to lower your voice and speak in a whisper when you enter. The lack of warmth and personality, the uncomfortable seating, the priceless antiques you're petrified of breaking. Obviously, all this is true of most bank buildings, too, not to mention investment firms: all the hard edges, polished marble and glass and metal surfaces, the divided, soundproofed offices, the mostly rectangular meeting tables.

This observation turned out to be a recurring theme in my conversations with other people of color working as funders. One colleague, an Asian American woman, took a job with a corporate foundation after being recruited at the age of 27. Her portfolio alone was $6 million to $8 million, with the whole place dispersing $30 million a year. She remembers her first day:

> I was wearing a business suit and really nice shoes, because the place was formal, business attire, very professional. I walked in and it's on the thirteenth floor, overlooking the water and the bridge. A view as beautiful as the day. I had a computer and my own office. And I was just like, "Holy crap. Have I arrived?" It was so quiet. And sterile. Not a lot of color, lots of gray. I just went in quietly and sat down in my office. My glass-walled office. I was used to working in basements and vans, around trash bags and vomit. It didn't compute.
>
> Of course, I was also kind of digging it, my own office where I could close my door and make my phone calls. It felt very special and also very scary. I didn't want to mess things up.[2]

A Latina colleague remembers her first impressions of the institution that hired her:

> It's set on a campus. There are deer hopping around. There was something about the place that makes you feel like you're entering a mausoleum. You almost want to whisper. I was like, "What is it about this that bothers me so much?" I couldn't place it for a long time. I think it's about wanting to silence reality to some extent. There is something powerful about the choice to physically remove yourself from the reality of the issues that you are working on. I couldn't name it at the moment, but it has stayed with me for a long, long time.[3]

You know there's a style of architecture called "colonial," right? It's not even one style; it encompasses all the examples of a colonizer's style of building and the materials used in building in the home country, transplanted to the colony, so there are French Colonial houses, Dutch Colonial, and Spanish Colonial. Embarrassingly for Britain, if there's no country named, a plain old colonial building can be assumed to refer to British style.

There's no doubt: most of institutions that move and control money exhibit colonial style. This is how the separation paradigm I mentioned in chapter 1 shows up in design and architecture.

Professional buildings intentionally feel different from spaces where people live. The cold, hard style and feel of these spaces allows the decisions made there to be impersonal and rigid, following rules rather than flexibly adapting to the complexity of human situations. Their location, architecture, and design support colonizing tactics of division, control, and exploitation, which is why I call these spaces "ivory towers."

Colonial Social Architecture

Just as the architects who were behind the physical space made design choices to reinforce the Us versus Them separation worldview, there also were architects of the *organizational design* who made choices that had serious consequences.

Organizational design determines fundamental elements like how power is held and by whom, who makes decisions and how decisions are carried out, the relationship of the organization to resources, and what constitutes success, effectiveness, purpose, and so on.

Most organizations and institutions operating in the world today, and particularly those that handle money, reflect the design principles of the social architects of the industrial revolution and the scientific revolution. They were mostly philosophers, economists, scientists, and statesmen working in the late 1700s through the early 1900s, almost exclusively white men who privileged the rational (the mind) over all else, intoxicated with the separation paradigm. When the philanthropic and social sectors were developed in the early part of the twentieth century, the design elements were the same: bureaucracy, competition, specialization, and consolidation of power and resources. Tradition and the status quo were worshipped, resulting in conformity, formality, and arrogance. In other words, separation, separation, and more separation.

"It's not hard to map the neocolonial DNA across our sector . . . the effect of concentrating power, hyperprofessionalizing in a way that creates exclusivity, co-opting existing culture, forcing assimilation, leveraging local populations to obtain resources, and reinforcing larger systems of oppression," write Stanford scholars Jess Rimington and Joanna Levitt Cea, who are cataloging the hallmarks of "colonized organizational design" in both the nonprofit and for-profit sectors.[4]

The social architects developed a strict hierarchy of authority, the pyramid model, in which the small number of the Us are perched at the very top, holding the authority and the vision. Pyramid processes are top-down, closed-door, and expert-driven. Populating the base of the pyramid, with the greatest numbers but the least power, were the Them—the Others, basically—less human and less valuable, due to receive fewer rights and resources. In between were middlemen (and middlewomen, though only more recently), who implemented the vision of the top and kept the bottom aligned to that vision.

Once these kinds of organizational structures became the norm, resources could be effectively extracted and consolidated for those at the top. The extracted and consolidated wealth was guarded and preserved for the Us and kept away from the Them, which further reinforced the division between Haves and Have-Nots. A particular type of ownership model grew dominant: the publicly traded corporation, in which shares of ownership are traded among the elite in the stock market. The extent of the wealth was often hidden, especially from those at the bottom of the pyramid. The fundamental dynamic is a one-way flow of resources—whether that means money, services, or information—from those more fortunate (the Haves) to the less fortunate (Have-Nots).

In these organizations, the experience of the least empowered people/roles—often relegated to less intellectual, more physical tasks—is that their time has less value and is therefore compensated with less pay. Their thoughts are also less valued, their voices discouraged. Their experience of work feels more anonymous, more interchangeable, less meaningful than the experience at the top of the pyramid. Their individuality and personal creative expression is likely not welcome in, and possibly is strictly prohibited from, the workplace.

Leadership as designed by these same architects reflected the "great man theory," where the leader is basically the alpha male. He is usually white and heterosexual, and compared with the other straight white men, he is the strongest, most educated, and most focused, ruthless and relentless in pursuing goals. He knows where to go, what to do, how to do it, and his followers understand their role simply as "follow his lead." This leadership style is rigid and transactional. The leader's commands must be followed, otherwise the consequences are discipline and punishment, so it's often called command-and-control leadership.

In their *Dismantling Racism* workbook, Kenneth Jones and Tema Okun identified other characteristics of white supremacy culture, including perfectionism, sense of urgency, defensiveness, quantity over quality, worship of the written word, paternalism, either/or thinking, fear of open conflict, individualism, worship of unlimited growth, objectivity, and avoidance of discomfort. They note:

> The characteristics . . . are used as norms and standards without being pro-actively named or chosen. . . . Organizations which unconsciously use these characteristics as their norms and standards make it difficult, if not impossible, to open the door to other cultural norms and standards. As a result, many of our organizations, while saying we want to be multicultural, really only allow other people and cultures to come in if they adapt or conform to already existing cultural norms.[5]

Colonial, white supremacist organizational practices seem inevitable because they were so universally adopted, and they still govern the great majority of our institutions, but they were *design choices*. This means that other choices are available, even when they seem far-fetched. We know what spaces and organizations look like, feel like, and function like when they are inspired by the colonizers' principles of separation, competition, and exploitation. How would they be different if they were based on principles like integration and interdependence, reciprocity and relationship?

CHAPTER THREE

House Slaves

How diversity efforts backfire and reinforce colonization

The president of the Kate B. Reynolds Charitable Trust was new. Never before in its history had the foundation chosen a woman to be president. She compelled me to come back for a second interview, and then a third. By the third, I was coming to terms with the job: *You're telling me that if I came to work here as a "program officer," I would basically be giving away 25 million dollars a year to whomever I think should get it. So what's the catch?*

After they had confirmed that I had no skeletons hidden in my closet and that I was just an honest-to-goodness Southern Christian boy, I was offered the job. I also had to agree to a code of conduct that included no public drunkenness or swearing, among other things.

I said yes, making me her first hire. Me, this little brown kid, just 28 years old, and usually taken for even younger. (I've got a small frame, and back then I was a 28 waist, too. Those were the days.)

Why did I take the job? I trusted my gut. Something within my heart told me that this was a good place for me to do God's work.

Also, the money. I signed on for $65,000, making me the highest-paid person in my graduating class; the residency programs in hospital management typically paid $40,000. It wasn't long before my salary was bumped up further, and only a couple of years before I was making six figures. For the first time in my life I felt financially secure. My salary was unimaginable for someone in my family. Not to mention the perks. The paid holidays! We'd have a very fancy holiday party around December 10, and then we were off until January 6 or 8. We just shut down the office, and got paid for it. Lots of vacation time. On top of the pay, we got a 10 percent bonus every paycheck, instead of having a retirement fund, because we had so few employees.

After one year there, I bought a beautiful brand-new house, because I'd listened to Oprah growing up, and she had driven home the message that home ownership was the anchor of wealth. I had subscribed to the American Dream.

When the foundation suggested that I get rid of my old Honda Civic because it didn't represent their image (the legacy of wealth), I went to the dealership to look at a nicer used car, but they had something less modest in mind for me: *Oh, no. You work at Kate B. Reynolds. You guys do such good work in the community.* They gave me an incredible deal on a brand-new Volvo S60, right out of the showroom. It was outside my budget, but they made it work. Now I was really living the dream.

That brings me to the other reason the job was irresistible: the prestige. I received automatic respect from the community. I knew the mayor of the town. My first Christmas, I received hundreds of Christmas cards, including one from the state governor—a real card that she actually signed. I'd roll up in my foundation-sponsored car (provided for business trips, so I got saved from putting miles on my new Volvo) for a site visit at the hospital in Southern Pines, a very wealthy neighborhood, and the CEO always met me at the front door. I couldn't help but think, *Wow, I am Somebody now.*

Everywhere I went I was catered to, even to an embarrassing degree. One time I casually mentioned that I liked to drink diet Dr Pepper. All of a sudden, our refrigerator in the office was stocked with diet Dr Pepper, although I was the only one in the office who drank it. Then I noticed that when I went out into the community for meetings, it was always available. *Why is there diet Dr Pepper everywhere? Is this the most popular drink now or what?* I asked someone, "Do you all drink diet Dr Pepper?" No, they had called my office and asked what I liked to drink. It was almost too much.

For the first time in my life, I could demand things of people, and I'd have my way. When my family needed medical care, I called ahead. *Mama, you give them my name.* And for the first time in her life she got first-class service everywhere. I can't say I wasn't proud.

~~~~~

A lot of people of color go into philanthropy and social finance for the same reasons I did. For many of us, it's about purpose: we earnestly hope, and sometimes believe, that we can connect the foundation's assets with our drive to improve outcomes for the planet and its people, especially people in our own communities.

"I get a role in deploying resources in a way that creates equity in communities that need more equitable outcomes. Even though I'm not white, working in philanthropy can give me some access to that white privilege," one colleague told me.[1]

Another colleague said, "I value community. I value close relationships with people. I value a strong sense of purpose, feeling like I'm making a difference."[2] A Black man from the South shared that he was recruited into philanthropy after—and because—he had spent a long time doing work in the very community that the foundation wanted to fund.

> I wasn't chasing a gig in philanthropy, that's for damn sure. I had worked on the other side for a decade and had interacted with foundations and donors throughout that entire time. With foundations it was usually challenging. I felt like I was often talking to people who . . . I don't know how to say it except that they were lost in their ego. It was because they were moving money, but it was money that wasn't theirs. They had no clue as to what was going on in my community, what we were really trying to accomplish, which further exaggerated the already weird power dynamic. There was no mutual respect in the relationship.

> But the person who recruited me was an exception, someone I did trust in philanthropy, who had been a good partner to me. As my program officer, she not only funded me, she kept in contact with me beyond the requirements of the grant. She created less distance between herself

and her grantee partners than most foundation program staff would do. Her foundation thought it would be helpful to have someone who was from the South, who was Black, who knew racial justice work in the South, to come run a portfolio that was designed to address racial justice issues in the South. So I said yes. Once I went over to the foundation side and became a peer as opposed to a grantee, my relationships with people in philanthropy completely changed. Everyone was nicer. They wanted to support my leadership.[3]

Many of us come into the work after doing public service or community organizing, as he had done, having experienced philanthropy from the "other side of the table," when we were seeking funding. Most of this grassroots work in our communities is compensated very poorly, and sometimes is even on a volunteer basis. So if we're honest about it, the pay and the prestige are also very compelling.

One colleague was recruited by a foundation when she was just 27. She and her family were refugees from Vietnam, and she learned English as her second language when they settled in Texas. The job offer came during a recession.

"I was poor; I was young. They were offering me $40,000 to $50,000, basically $30,000 more than I was making. I needed literally to make rent, I had no assets, maybe $400 in my checking account. And I was hungry to be in a place where I had a tiny bit more authority than where I had been before."[4]

As another Black colleague put it, "The only reason I entertained the offer is because they pay, and nobody else paid."[5]

Tokens and Model Minorities

So that's why I took the job, why we all took the jobs. But why were we hired?

It should go without saying that I was qualified for the job. I came from a great university program—the University of North Carolina at Chapel Hill was among the best. And it was just over an hour away, so the university and the foundation knew people in common who knew and vouched for me. Also, I had valuable, relevant experience—while completing my studies I'd been working for seven years with a national nonprofit organization that did health advocacy work.

On top of that, the new president was deliberate about wanting to diversify the staff in terms of age and race/ethnicity. Ah, diversity. It's one of those words that's been stretched and diluted until it's come to mean too much, and then not much of anything at all. "Diversity" is how white people talk about race when they don't want to talk about race, but it also can mean the representation of any marginalized group, including Indigenous people, women, queer folk, people with disabilities, immigrants, and people of particular religious or ethnic backgrounds. It can mean people with different mindsets and values, or people of different ages and people from different parts of the country.

For the foundation, I checked a lot of boxes, being a Native American—often taken for Latino—but a Native who dresses, speaks, and behaves in a mainstream way. And in terms of increasing age diversity, I sure was young, relative to the field. I was the youngest program officer in North Carolina—and I was among the youngest in the country.

Foundations and financial institutions let a few token people of color in, because they see that we have a different quality of access to our communities and because we have some type of wisdom that they want, but we're expected to completely assimilate. Imagine you married into a very wealthy family that is all about keeping up appearances. You are expected to conform to their behavior and their way of acting and interacting and moving through the world. That's what it's like. They will view you the way Rose's mother (played by Frances Fisher) stared at Jack (played by Leonardo DiCaprio) in the movie *Titanic*. She "looked at him like an insect. A dangerous insect which must be squashed quickly." (Yes, I saw the movie 12 times in 1998.) If you contradict them, you will be reviled or silenced. If you bring your full self to work, they will push you out. If you reveal any of the craziness or dark secrets that run in the family, they will excommunicate you.

Tokens end up on tiptoe, always on our best behavior. This is heightened by the sense that we still often have the feeling that we are representing our entire race, that everything we do will reflect on all other Latinos or Blacks or Asian Americans or Natives. Who's going to speak truth to power when there could be negative consequences for everyone who looks like you, not just in this moment but into the foreseeable future?

A Black colleague admitted:

> By my fourth day, I had already begun to regret taking the job. . . . The truth is, I've never felt quite like I could bring my full self to the job. I never felt like I could speak freely. I feel like I have to play a role. I myself have become more conservative in how I operate. Not in my thinking, but how I move through the world. It's almost like an expectation that you yourself get in line. Not even

an expectation—it's required. You have to assimilate in order to be able to move anything inside of
a foundation. You have to drink the Kool-Aid and
operate like they do, move like they do.[6]

"I feel hyper-self-consciousness when I enter very
white spaces," a Latina colleague says. "I am very aware of
my hands moving, my accent. I am very aware of it. Even
if I am proud of it, I'm still very aware of it."[7] Another colleague told me,

> I was scared shitless because I had just left an
> organization where I "played the race card too
> early" and had shot myself in the foot as a result.
> So I basically kept my head down, working hard
> for about a year before I did anything that revealed
> anything about me personally. Looking back, I
> was trying to build unassailable credibility and
> just be really, really good at the work.[8]

Yet another colleague says, "I'm always trying to play
that game of chess of what are they expecting from me as
an Asian American woman, as somebody who's kind of
midlevel professional, and where do I push some of the
assumptions versus where do I not rock the boat because I
just make things harder for myself?"[9]

Gerri Spilka, Vivian Figueredo, and Georgia Kioukis
note, "According to authors Rebecca Stone and Benjamin
Butler, in *Core Issues in Comprehensive Community-Building
Initiatives: Exploring Power and Race* and in *Structural
Racism and Community Building*, foundations may unwit-
tingly perpetuate a dominant worldview, one that is highly
racialized and often dictated by white European culture. In
an organizational environment governed by the dominant

worldview, individuals are prone to making decisions from an ethnocentric vantage point."[10]

A common way the leadership in philanthropy conveys its doubt in our ability and credibility is to bring in independent consultants to research the very issues that we have intimate knowledge of from our time living in and/or working with communities on the ground. It was this very expertise for which we were often hired. As expressed by a Black colleague from the South:

> We had to hire a consulting firm the last six months to do a full scan of [the field], just to bring it back to my boss and to his boss to say everything that I've been saying for the last year. Literally the report is verbatim all of the stuff that I had brought up, but no one heard it, or it wasn't given the same weight without having some sort of outside, external person who was paid a lot of money to say it and put it nice and neatly down on paper. That's the game that we're forced to play.[11]

His experience was echoed by an investigation commissioned by the Association of Black Foundation Executives, which looked into a concerning trend: the inability of the philanthropic sector to hold on to Black employees. ABFE's investigation culminated in a 2014 report called *The Exit Interview*, which found that many Black professionals left because they felt extra scrutinized and their expertise was not trusted.[12]

An Asian American colleague talks about the frequent assumption or intimation that the (only) grantmaker of color from a given community has an unprofessional personal agenda. She's been called "righteous" ("and not in a good way," she quips) for defending her recommendation to fund organizations led by people of color. It's a double-edged sword, she says: "When it's convenient for a foundation, they'll parade around the diversity and say, 'Look, we reflect the wider community.' But then our conundrum becomes *How do we advocate for our community without being accused of becoming too passionate, of playing favorites?*"[13]

I also felt I had to do acrobatics around staying "objective and professional," not seeming to favor Native American grantseekers. Of course, this is exactly what championing equity involves, so it's a ridiculous and strenuous expectation. I had to do a lot of extra explaining to give myself credibility, especially to our all-white board and to the good old boy network among our grantees, who at first seemed incredulous that a boyish brown man was holding the key to their treasure box.

When, upon getting a job in an ivory tower, you are made to feel like you won the lottery, part of what is communicated to you is that there are many, many others ready to take your place. You're replaceable. And there are only so many "designated minority" positions to go around. That position can easily be reallocated to another "poor and needy" candidate to keep the quota filled. It's a subtle way to keep you behaving well, assimilating into the culture, working like a dog. Whether or not it is deliberate, as the only one of our kind, we often hear how lucky we are to work in this esteemed and powerful field. *Boy, you were given the chance of a lifetime!*

Now, there is no doubt it is a privilege to work in a field that controls and moves money, whether it's banking or investing or philanthropy. It is. I don't want to take away that it is. I just want to say that I feel like it's a privilege for these fields to have me, too.

Foundations often seek out young "model minorities" like me who are the first in our families to "make it." Yet here's the thing about institutions—or any systems, really—that were created by and for a certain kind of person (white straight men, say) that then decide they want to "be inclusive" or "open their doors to diversity" or "commit to equity": having a seat at the table is not the same as feeling free to speak in your own voice, to offer your own divergent ideas, to bring your full self to bear on the work.

~~~~

To be clear, most of us are still "token" Others in an almost pure-white world. The statistics are dismal regarding the number of white men versus Others inside the ivory tower institutions controlling wealth. Three-fourths of foundations' full-time staff is white. According to the Council on Foundations *2020 Grantmaker Salary and Benefits Report*, only about a third of program officers (34.8 percent) and about 10 percent of foundation CEOs are people of color. Only 4 percent of philanthropic institutions are led by Black chief executives, with even more dismal representation for other races and ethnicities.[14]

Board leadership is even more demographically starved. "Fully 85 percent of foundation board members are white, while just 7 percent are African American and only 4 percent are Hispanic," says Gara LaMarche, the former president of the Democracy Alliance. "Nearly three-quarters of foundations have no written policy on board diversity."[15] When I joined the board of the Andrus Family Fund in 2017, I was one of only two Native Americans on a national private foundation board. Since then, I've heard of only one additional appointment—and that was on a regional foundation board.

Along the rest of the loans-to-gifts spectrum, the C-suite of financial services is 90 percent white, with attrition (dropout) rates higher and rates of promotion lower for people of color, so although entry-level positions show more racial diversity, it disappears in the executive tiers.[16] When it comes to venture capital, the disparities are also stark: 70 percent of venture capitalists are white and 82 percent are male. Most of the 30 percent of nonwhite VCs are Asian American. Just 3 percent are Black—not really a surprise, when only four of the Fortune 500 companies have Black CEOs—and 1 percent are Latino. No one even mentions the numbers for Native Americans.[17] Minority angel investors make up less than 13 percent of total angel investors.[18]

And then there's humanitarian aid. In a 2008 article called "The New Colonialists" in *Foreign Policy*, the authors critique the "hodgepodge of international charities, aid agencies, philanthropists, and foreign advisers" who "are increasingly taking over key state functions, providing for the health, welfare, and safety of citizens" in many so-called developing nations. They continue:

> In much the same way European empires once dictated policies across their colonial holdings, the new colonialists—among them international development groups such as Oxfam, humanitarian nongovernmental organizations (NGOs) like Doctors Without Borders and Mercy Corps, and mega-philanthropies like the Bill & Melinda Gates Foundation—direct development strategies and craft government policies for their hosts. But though the new colonialists are the glue holding society together in many weak states, their

presence often deepens the dependency of these states on outsiders.[19]

Mother Jones quoted the head of the diversity office at the Consumer Financial Protection Bureau as saying, "There's certainly a thought that if you have a more diverse workforce and if you have a more diverse group of suppliers, that institutions very well could do a better job of understanding a more diverse marketplace and how to best serve it."[20] Yes, and while the numbers should be cause for alarm, a focus on just balancing out the numbers is not enough. Diversity statistics that get held up as a sole measure of progress are an insufficient measure, because we need to go beyond mere representation, to access to power and ownership.

#diversityfails

In philanthropy, there have been dozens of initiatives on diversity, equity, and inclusion, often lumped together using the acronym DEI. The field has spent hundreds of thousands, maybe millions, on making these buzzwords the subject of conference topics, task forces, summits, surveys, reports, and trainings. Vu Le, a nonprofit leader who frequently writes and speaks about the sector, using humor to point out a lot of our stuck places and particular afflictions, describes the hot air:

> When we just talk about Equity and go no further, we are guilty of Fakequity. . . . People seem to think that forming an equity committee, talking about equity, sending staff and board to trainings, "listening" to communities, conducting research and gathering data, and adding terminologies to

websites and brochures are sufficient to achieving equity. But no, these things are necessary, but not sufficient.[21]

A Latina colleague summed it up: "I always want to stab myself in the eye with a pencil because it is the same old conversation."[22]

One of the colleagues I interviewed was asked to form what ultimately wound up being named the DICE committee: "We couldn't decide on the title. Some people wanted diversity. Some wanted inclusion, others equity. Some wanted cultural humility, so we decided to throw it all in the pot because I got tired of meeting after meeting just devoted to naming ourselves instead of doing the work."[23]

Another colleague recalls a diversity initiative that was launched at her workplace. The organizers led her and her colleagues through the exercise commonly called the "privilege walk," where everyone starts in one line in the middle of the room and you step forward or step back based on what kind of barriers or privileges you have encountered in life. For example, "Take a step back if anyone in your family's ever been incarcerated. . . . Step forward if you grew up with more than five books in the house. . . . Step back if you've ever been a victim of violence," and so on.

An African American guy, a friend of mine, and I, we started stepping back. And with every question we kept stepping back. It only took eight questions for us to hit the back wall. And they kept asking questions and we couldn't step back any further. It was like the pit of inequality. It was so deep that we just sat down. There wasn't enough space in the room to physically show how many barriers we had overcome to get to where we were. Everyone else was towards the middle or the very front of the room. Some people were so far in front that they couldn't go forward any further. It was a big room, but not big enough for their privilege.

It brought up all kinds of feelings. Was I just a pity party?

Would all of us in that room who had to keep working together just pretend like we hadn't seen how different our lives had been to get to this same place?

What is the toll of being public and proud about how long the road has been, about your determination and resilience and grit?

What's the emotional and psychological toll it takes to educate others about what privilege means?

How far can resilience stretch when there's continuous retraumatization—at what point do the psyche and the soul just shatter?[24]

It is undeniably difficult for people of color to be successful in the ivory tower institutions of wealth. The few of us who have pushed through and stayed for more than a decade have learned to coach each other through all the racism, the weirdness, the guilt, the uncomfortable power dynamics. Possibly we were fortunate enough to land in an environment where we could be a little bit more true to who we are.

What we know is that talk—meaning everything from conducting research to holding sensitivity trainings to writing formal policies—is not enough, whether it's talk about diversity, equity, or inclusion. Sometimes all the talk is outright counterproductive. Studies show that it can activate bias, create resentment, or spark a backlash (or a "whitelash"). In fact, despite all of the dollars and hours invested in efforts inside philanthropy, the newest data from the Council on Foundations shows that the number of people of color and the number of women in philanthropy have actually decreased.[25] Studies also show that efforts to support diversity in corporate settings are often counterproductive, because the approach follows more of the same divisive, dominating colonial tactics. "Your organization will become less diverse, not more, if you require managers to go to diversity training, try to regulate their hiring and promotion decisions, and put in a legalistic grievance system," wrote Frank Dobbin and Alexandra Kalev in the *Harvard Business Review* in 2016, calling this the "classic command-and-control approach to diversity."[26]

Diversity talk allows people to deny racism. It lets white folks ignore persistent, alarming racial inequalities and discriminatory policies and practices. It lets people off the hook about their responsibility in maintaining a colonial white supremacist society. Andrea Armeni, the executive director of Transform Finance, calls "diversity and inclusion" initiatives "false solutions" to inequity and injustice:

> Having some managers of color is definitely a step in the right direction, and a very much needed one. But that doesn't, per se, bring us anywhere towards racial justice. Looking at how many people of color are on the board or in top management of a corporation doesn't really tell me about whether, at large, communities of color are benefiting. You could have Halliburton run by African Americans; it's still not necessarily a racially just organization.[27]

~~~

Why should *ivory towers hire people like me?* This is a good question.

Those most excluded and exploited by today's broken economy possess exactly the perspective and wisdom needed to fix it. Ironically, the separation paradigm that locked us out and made us Others actually cultivated our resilience strategies. To survive the trauma of exploitation, we always had to believe that the dominant worldview was only one option, even when it seemed ubiquitous and inevitable. This has made us masters of alternative possibilities.

In their intoxicated rush to consolidate wealth, colonizers reduced the number of religions, languages, species, cultures, social systems, media channels, and political systems. On all scales, global to local, this homogenizing campaign—*global bleaching*, you could call it—made the world not just more bland and boring but also less innovative and less resilient. Evolution and innovation arise from difference and variation, not from sameness. These are fundamental principles of life. For us to have carried inside ourselves the possibility or even hope of a different world is powerful all by itself.

More concretely speaking, we who are Others translate effectively between the world of the funder and the world of those seeking funding, because we ourselves have to switch between worlds all the time. "Code-switching" is the term linguists adopted to describe switching between more than one language in a conversation, but it also has come to mean the shift between cultures, as revealed in word choice, accents, and styles of expression. A classic example is the Southerner who hides his accent when he goes to work in a Manhattan law firm. It's particularly common among people of color and colonized people.

Over our lifetimes, nonwhite people learn to smoothly transition between the language of the powerful—standard "white" English—and our cultural dialects. We constantly make split-second choices about our cadences and inflections and expressions, based on with whom we are talking. We hold back our most authentic expressions of our self, whether in language, clothing, or the stories we share, waiting to first see if it feels safe to do so. We become expert navigators of difference, cultivating this level of awareness in a way our white colleagues, especially the monolingual ones, never have to. It's a burden, but it's also a superpower, as it turns out.

Chris Cardona, a colleague at the Ford Foundation whose parents were immigrants from Colombia, grew up around his *abuelitos* (grandparents) in Colombia and, later, with godparents in Massachusetts, whom he called Grandma and Grandpa. "Bridging is something I think that many Latinos have," he says. "Language shapes the way that we understand and interact with the world, and having access to more than one language provides a broader set of perspectives. You can see different realities and connect them."[28]

Working with people who are different from you, in a culture that is not your own, using language that is not the way you naturally express yourself—these challenges push your brain to expand its habitual ways of thinking and sharpen its performance. "Boundary spanning" is another way of describing this capacity, and it's often considered a specialty of those of us outside the dominant culture. This also tends to make us particularly skilled at coalition building, specifically the ability to come together around common ground despite differing identities. We often possess the ability to hold multiple realities simultaneously;

our thinking unifies, contains, and transcends oppositions, a stance that's really needed in the current divided and divisive sociocultural-political climate.

Talking about the entrepreneurs of color who get just 1 percent of funding, consultant Ryan Bowers commented,

> They're usually even stronger because they're so risk averse. They're so bootstrapped, and they've had to carry the stuff on their backs and put their own dollars into it. They don't have access to friends and family dollars to raise that initial seed round. These are folks that have had to work way harder, way more meticulously, be way more careful. That's exactly who you want. That's the resilient investment that you want to make.[29]

Until now, diversity and inclusion tactics have been about getting different kinds of people in the door and then asking them to assimilate to the dominant white colonizer culture. But the issue is not recruitment of diverse humans—the "pipeline" focus of the past, or "laying a seat at the table," as it is often said. The issue is creating a culture of respect, curiosity, acceptance, and love. It's about fundamentally changing organizational culture, what constitutes acceptable behavior, and the definitions of success and leadership. It's about building ourselves a whole new table—one where we truly belong.

CHAPTER FOUR

Field Hands

How granting funds and loans to those who seek it can feel good . . . but still reinforce colonial dynamics

One day a woman seeking funding for a domestic violence shelter arrived at the Kate B. Reynolds office for a meeting with me. Because she had come from so far away, the other side of the state practically, she had driven to Winston-Salem the day before our appointment and spent the night in a hotel in order to meet with me the next day. I didn't know that, or anything about her or the organization, because at that point we didn't do any screening on the phone. Unless someone was a previous grantee, I walked in blind, with no history or information. I would see that process change during my tenure, but for this woman, those changes hadn't come soon enough. I felt just terrible when this woman said that she had driven up the previous day and spent the night at a hotel. We could have had a 10-minute phone call to determine whether she was eligible, instead, and saved her the hassle.

To put grantseekers at ease, I usually started with casual conversation. I tried to get on their wavelength. I might talk a little more "country" with them, depending on where in the state they were from. I asked her how the drive had been and she said, "I left the hotel two hours ago to make sure I didn't get lost in this big city, Winston-Salem. Then I got in a car wreck."

From bad to worse. "I am so sorry," I said. "Are you okay?"

"Actually, I feel like I hurt my back," she told me. "I'm in some pain, but I wasn't going to miss this appointment with you, Mr. Edgar."

Oh God, this was terrible. Worse yet, the minute she started talking about the work she was doing and what she was seeking funding for, I knew it was something that we didn't fund. It was tragic. I heard her out anyway and tried to figure out if I could send her on to any other foundations, to make the whole catastrophic trip worth her time.

As we were wrapping up, she looked up at the wall and saw my diploma from Jackson College of Ministries.

"I didn't know that you were a minister."

"Well, I'm not really," I told her, "but I did go to seminary."

She was not taking no for an answer. "No, you are a minister. I knew there was something about you." She started getting excited. "Can I ask you a favor? Will you lay hands on me and pray for my back? I believe God can use you right now and my back can be healed."

Of course I said yes. There was nothing I wouldn't have done for this woman, given the situation, no matter how uncomfortable it made me. Luckily, I already had the door to the office closed because she was a loud talker. So I now stretched out my hand and placed it on her arm, but she took my hand and moved it to the top of her head. *Dear God, don't let anyone walk in my office right now.* I was worried the secretary would come and stick her head in to say my next appointment was there.

Loud enough so she could hear, but as quietly as possible to prevent my colleagues from hearing, I prayed, "Dear God, I pray that you help this sister and you take this pain away. Let there be a speedy recovery."

She started praying with me, affirming as I spoke. "Yes, Lord. Yes, Lord! *Yes, Lord!*" She got louder and louder and louder.

I wanted her to be free of that pain, but I was freaking out about someone coming in and seeing me laying my hands on this woman like a zealous evangelist at a tent revival. Then she started really feeling the Spirit. She literally started shaking and began to have a full, flat-out Holy Ghost visitation right there in my office. I recognized it from my Pentecostal upbringing. She may have even spoken in tongues, I don't remember. Tears streamed down her face.

"*Yes, Jesus!*" she shouted.

Finally the moment subsided and she got ready to go.

At least she got the Spirit, I thought with relief, since she wasn't getting a grant. That was something. Maybe God did use me in that moment to facilitate her healing. Doing that work, there were moments I felt I was operating in the flow or in the Spirit. Usually, it was when I could give people money they desperately needed.

~~~~

When I arrived, that was the process at Kate B. Reynolds. There was an open invitation for organizations from the state of North Carolina to apply. That sounded good at first, open and fair. But KBR required that people meet with us in person before they applied. They had to come to us like we were the Wizard of Oz bestowing gifts. There was no telephone screening first to help determine eligibility. Most days at the office were filled with back-to-back meetings with these folks seeking funding. There was a waiting area, and although it was of course finely furnished and comfortable, it was awkward for people to see each other there, given they were essentially competing against one another for funding.

The foundation divided responsibilities by geography; each of the program officers covered part of the state. I handled approximately 80 grants per cycle—or per docket, as we say in the biz. My days were filled with meeting, meeting, meeting, meeting, meeting, and then deciding on a slew of grants. I had to pull multiple long weekends to write up my recommendations. It was a lot of work.

I had power in the selection process, basically making a recommendation on who should get funded or not get funded. If I wanted to say no, I could find a way. If you didn't complete your application, I could deliberately not follow up with you to get the rest of the material. If I really wanted to fund you but you didn't do a good job answering the questions, I could call and dig for more information. I could do the extra work to try to get it to a yes. I searched out organizations and people in the community who were really doing great work. I had the power to help them navigate the system.

I put together the short list and then presented, or sometimes defended, my decision in front of the team, my president, and our advisory board. The executive board, mostly employees of Wachovia (which is now Wells Fargo), had the final approval of all grants, as the bank was the sole corporate trustee. Our advisory board members were all white, and all but one were men. Many of them were also grantees, representatives of large health care systems. That kind of conflict of interest is fairly run-of-the-mill in the world of philanthropy, I would come to learn. If we had a grant pending with a board member's institution, which we pretty much did every cycle, of course we would fund that.

In general, because of our culture of politeness, and out of respect for the due diligence that the staff had done, the board rarely would say no to the staff's recommendations. Between the Southern culture and the philanthropy culture, there was a lot of niceness, no rocking the boat. I learned how to present my recommendations in a way that was compliant, and that was really the only thing they cared about—compliance. *Don't break the law* was essentially their guiding principle. There wasn't a whole lot of pushback.

Still, there were several times where I really wanted to fund something, and I knew their heart was in the right place, but I just could not sell it. The grantseekers didn't give me enough, or it was a little bit too much of a stretch for the foundation's culture. I routinely brought those kinds of proposals in, if only to create the space to have the conversation and to try to push their thinking. One time they overturned a grant that I had recommended for a yes, for an organization that was doing advocacy work. When you went to the organization's website, it screamed lobby and legislation, and it scared the board, so they overturned it. I guess I can't blame them for that one.

The hardest part of the job was having to say no to someone seeking funding for truly good work in their community, based on the sometimes arbitrary rules and regulations of the foundation. Over time, I learned that I had to be careful about the signs I gave folks, even unconsciously.

As Chris Cardona of the Ford Foundation put it:

> I've come to learn—sometimes the hard way—the weight that your words carry as a philanthropy professional. As informally and accessibly as you

try to carry yourself, I've experienced that folks interpret what you're saying and parse it for signals about potential funding. If you're not careful, that can produce disappointment or even harm. That gives me a different kind of pause than I had before. It's probably fair to say that makes me more risk averse with how I communicate. Even to highlight one particular grantee's work can send a signal that I didn't intend. Given the volume of requests, inquiries, and interest we receive as philanthropy professionals, it takes an adjustment to manage relationships responsibly, to manage expectations. It ends up being a big part of the work, both externally and internally.[1]

What Seeking Funds Feels Like

Imagine going to the doctor and explaining at length your symptoms and the gravity of your situation. Your condition is hard to classify, involving intersections of body, mind, and environment, but the doctor forces you to choose a single label for it, even though it's not accurate. You have to fill out a pile of paperwork. Finally the doctor sends you away, saying, "Okay, we're going to review your case and decide *if* we will help you." As you leave, you eye the crowd of afflicted people in the waiting room, knowing that only some of the people will get help. In this intense climate of scarcity and competition, you can't help but look at some of them and think, *They don't seem that sick at all; they don't seem like they need the help as much as I do.* Then you go away with your pain and you wait months for an answer. And if you do get the help, you are made to understand that you will have to display improvements within 12 months.

If you don't follow the doctor's extensive and confusing regulations to the letter, you might never get help again.

I interviewed a colleague who worked at Amnesty International, "a mostly white organization that does work mostly on behalf of people of color," she notes. "There's a little bit of savior syndrome baked into the DNA of the entire organization." An African American herself, she was invited into fundraising activities when the organization set out to cultivate more Black donors. "So . . . as a token," she says. She described the weird, uncomfortable dynamics:

> The process of getting funding and reporting back about the results is a draining process. It can be a demeaning process. I've been corrected by a white funder for saying "Black folks" instead of "African American" or "African diaspora." I've been corrected to not say "poor people." I was supposed to say "low income."

> When it comes time for a site visit from a funder, I have to stand there and smile and speak to the experience of Black folks, shucking and jiving. That's what we say when site visits come up: "It's time to shuck and jive." There's something about site visits and the questions that funders ask that isn't always about the work. It doesn't feel like a space to talk honestly about what's working well and what isn't working well, because the risk that comes with being totally honest and transparent is losing funding.

> Fundraising takes our time away from the work, and it sometimes subtly and not so subtly directs our work. We have to walk the line between trying to get funders to feel good about funding the work

that we're already doing on the one hand and making sure that funders feel like they're funding the work that they want to fund. It can be a tough line to walk, and the pressure, the burden is on us and not on the funders, so it doesn't really feel like the partnership that they claim it is.

Program officers, because they're not really ever on the ground in the community that they're funding, they don't know who's legitimate and who's not legitimate. Who should be getting the money? Who's really doing the work versus which organizations are writing really great reports with lots of pictures but they aren't moving the dial? The reality is that healing communities and building power, it takes time, and that doesn't fit with their ideal return on investment.[2]

None of this was news to me. I've heard it from countless grantees. It shouldn't be news to any funder, if they're listening. (Hint: they're not listening.)

Like all investors, foundations have their logic models, their strategic plans, and their theories of change, all of which are too often not applicable to the real world. They believe what they want to believe. Fund seekers are forced to play games, dangling projects that they know have "sex appeal" or reflect the trendy buzzword of the moment, in order to entice foundations to fund them. Many foundations simply will not fund an organization's existing work. For a long time, funders have also leaned away from general operating support—always the most helpful type of grant, because it can be applied to all facets of an organization's work as opposed to a single program—although this has finally been shifting in recent years.

It is rare that a funder acknowledges intersectionality, the fact that institutions and identities consist of and are impacted by overlapping and interconnected systems of oppression and disadvantage. Most funding is still stuck in issue-based silos. An education foundation will only fund education, a health foundation will only fund health, and so on, even though we know that every complex social problem has its roots everywhere—the environment, urban design, schools, diet, access to transport, as well as historical and cultural factors. Nevertheless, those seeking funds still must bend over backwards to fit themselves into a foundation's funding area.

A lot of foundations are lazy, funding the usual suspects, which most often are white-led organizations adept at creating glossy promotional materials and/or whose leaders have extensive Rolodexes that grant them more access to funders. The funding process is plagued by the cult of personality. "Funders have traditionally preferred the narrative of a rock star leader, and have invested in individuals more than in missions," comments adrienne maree brown, in her book *Emergent Strategy*.

> The shiny stars are rarely the ones actually getting the work done, or even doing the most exciting thinking in the organization. If you are in the funding world and your primary relationship with those you fund is with the executive director, if you have not had a meaningful conversation with other staff members or community members, you may be stricken with charismitis—relational laziness induced by charismatic brilliance.[3]

Many groups that are actually based in disadvantaged communities and led by locals are told, "You don't have the data; you don't have the track record; you're not big enough; you're not scalable; you don't align with the strategies we crafted after spending two years on strategic planning," as Vu Le puts it.[4]

As another colleague said,

> We hide behind this idea that we're being rigorous and being objective in our grant review, really at the same time creating barriers for smaller organizations, for people-of-color-led organizations. For example, when we ask, *Does the organization have more than three months of cash on hand? What organizations are going to be more likely to have those resources?*, these are things that we do that actually perpetuate inequity.[5]

Laborious applications and reporting requirements also keep some worthy groups from applying.

In 2004, the Applied Research Center, a racial justice think tank now known as Race Forward, found that grants aimed at communities of color averaged between 9 percent and 10 percent of all foundation funding in the 1990s.[6] In 2014, only 7.4 percent of all philanthropy (from individuals as well as institutions) was given for people of color, while foundation funding focused on reaching people of color has never exceeded 8.5 percent, according to a report by the Philanthropic Initiative for Racial Equity.[7] The proportion of money given specifically for African Americans and Natives actually decreased between 2005 and 2014. Despite changing demographics and increased societal awareness of the impacts of systemic racism, there has been no progress on expanding funding for people of color. Again according to the Philanthropic Initiative for Racial Equity, of all grantmaking in the United States, only 10 percent benefited people of color.[8]

Although there's a lot of talk about collaboration between grantees—combining forces rather than duplicating efforts—it's still relatively rare that a foundation explicitly funds such collaboration and funds it adequately. Foundations aren't providing "glue funding" to help hold coalitions together, because it takes extra work to make collaborative decisions, to attend all the coalition meetings, and to loop everyone in.

Finally, there's the absurd contradiction that grantmakers tend to be very slow in collecting proposals and making their funding decisions, on the one hand—although there are occasionally flare-ups of "rapid response grants" in the wake of disasters—while, on the other hand, they expect grantees to be able to show outcomes within a year or, at most, several years. Given the complexity of many issues that may have their origin in centuries' worth of root causes, this expectation is just plain crazy.

~~~~

KBR was a traditional place. The president was filling the shoes of a beloved longtime predecessor. She won my deepest respect when she started systematically changing the culture. She started redecorating the place not long after she arrived, painting the white walls purple, changing the blinds to colorful window treatments, replacing the heavy antique furniture with modern pieces. There was a lot of gasping and clutching of pearls in response. It may sound superficial, but it was symbolic of the larger cultural changes that ultimately had deep impacts on the community.

We brainstormed changes in the process around how we funded and who we funded. As a program officer, I took care of implementing the strategy changes in the day-to-day work. The president was ultimately the person who had to sell it to the board. I didn't envy her in that role. It must have been incredibly stressful, especially since she was the first woman in that position.

One big shift was to move a percentage of the money we granted into preventative health care, away from treatment. Essentially, we wanted to move away from the focus on hospitals and large institutions that had access to capital and focus on other levers of change that impacted health. It was hard to get excited about giving $200,000 toward Duke University Medical Center's $10 million budget for an emergency room. Duke was going to get there without us. Instead, we wanted to focus our investment more at the root cause of health problems, whether that was obesity prevention, smoking cessation, or domestic violence prevention. We also wanted to fund smaller, community-based organizations led by local leaders, often people of color, that developed specific, customized solutions inside their local communities.

It wasn't easy to make that change; it didn't go over without a fight. The head of the North Carolina Hospital Association—the state lobby for hospitals—was on our advisory board, and he objected when we said we wanted to pull away from funding so many hospitals. He pounded the table with his fists and yelled, "The charter of this foundation says to fund hospitals. We are moving away from its intent."

The foundation's leadership and I also worked to shift the foundation's transactional way of doing business and make it more relational. There were many small local groups doing wonderful work that were not applying to KBR for whatever reason. We needed to reach them. When I came on board, the program officer job description mostly entailed reading proposals and making recommendations.

It was completely transactional. I asked permission to rewrite the job descriptions. I wanted the work to be about engaging the community, going out to find excellent groups that were not on our radar, with a goal of bringing in three to five new proposals per docket.

I remember the president asking me, "You want to be held accountable for that?"

"Yes."

So we did it. We changed the job descriptions and actually put program officers on the road.

Previously, as I mentioned, grantseekers had to come to us. There was no screening beforehand; as a grantseeker you would just call and say, "I'm from such and such organization, I'd like to make an appointment." Except for the ones in the good old boys network, grantseekers and even prior grantees who came to our office were nervous, like it was a job interview. When the good old boys came in, we would slap backs and drink tea and exchange gossip and talk about their work, or I might drive over to Duke University, where a fruit basket and flowers waited in my hotel room, and eat a steak lunch with the senior executives.

As KBR moved away from the good old boys network and opened the doors for more small, grassroots groups and communities of color, the dynamic changed. Rather than having them come to our offices on the imposing, intimidating Reynolda campus, we went to them, after screening them first on the phone for basic eligibility. This entailed my driving out into rural North Carolina, spending hours on the road and staying at the Hampton Inn, far from glamorous.

I appreciated KBR for being willing to make those strategic changes, to get out of the ivory tower and into the community, and to take a risk on some new grantees.

However, none of the changes we made did anything about the core dynamics. The basis of traditional philanthropy is to preserve wealth, and all too often that wealth is fundamentally money that's been twice stolen, once through the colonial-style exploitation of natural resources and cheap labor and then a second time through tax evasion. Mostly white saviors and experts use this hoarded wealth to dominate and control—obviously or subtly—the seekers and recipients of those funds.

Dynamics of Power

The power dynamic is essentially the same among other kinds of lenders and investors, where the diversity numbers look even worse than in philanthropy. Among borrowers, minorities seeking loans are more heavily scrutinized and are given less support and assistance than their white peers. Minority-owned firms are three times more likely than white-owned firms to be denied loans. The average Black-owned firm obtains just $35,205 in total startup capital during its first year, compared with $106,720 for the average white-owned firm.[9] And this despite the Community Reinvestment Act of 1977, which requires lending in low-income communities.

Even with "friends and family funding," the support that comes early in the game, when things are still at the crazy idea stage, there are disparities. Those supporters are relatives, but they also come from alumni groups, professional connections, and social networks. Friends and family funding "accounts for more than $60 billion in small business investment every year. In fact, 38 percent of startup founders report raising money from their friends and family, with each venture raising capital of $23,000 on average," says Jessica Norwood of Runway. Unless, that is, you're talking about entrepreneurs of color. "On average, African American families have $11,000 in net worth, while white families have $141,900. As a result, the great ideas of many African American entrepreneurs never leave the napkin, because their networks simply can't provide the funds to launch a business," Jessica says. "Under current economic conditions, it would take 228 years for the average African American family to accumulate the wealth of an average white family today."[10]

Daryn Dodson, formerly a funds manager at Calvert Funds and now the managing partner of Illumen Capital, which does impact investing, has looked at the bias in investing. He collaborated with psychologist Jennifer Eberhardt, a MacArthur "Genius Grant" winner, who uncovered racial bias in the justice system. Eberhardt found that bias began at school, where Black boys were being expelled at four times the rate of their white peers for the exact same infractions, contributing to the education gap between races. Dodson found the same thing happening in investment.

When it comes to venture capital financing, the disparities are even starker: only 2.6 percent of VC funds went to African American and Latinx entrepreneurs in 2020.[11] In the social finance "doing well by doing good" space, which focuses on ventures that benefit people and solve social or environmental challenges first and make a profit second, the crowd is overwhelmingly white.

"The white folks in social finance feel more comfortable investing in some sustainable opportunity in Africa than they feel investing in African Americans," commented an African American consultant with whom I chatted at the 2017 SOCAP conference, the largest gathering in the social finance space.

There's an overlord mentality: they don't trust
Black or brown entrepreneurs to handle money.
Instead they move the money through one of the
intermediary organizations in this space, which
are mostly white-led. We've seen some of these
white-led intermediaries actually steal the ideas of
nonwhite entrepreneurs and launch it themselves.
The young white dude could just make a couple
calls, steal the intellectual capital and claim it for
himself, and raise money just like that.[12]

At the same time, higher interest rates and worse-qual-
ity loans tend to go to people of color. "African American
and Latino borrowers were about 30 percent more likely
to receive the highest-cost subprime loans relative to
white subprime borrowers with similar risk profiles,"
noted a report from the Center for Responsible Lending,
while "African Americans and Latinos are, respectively,
47 percent and 45 percent more likely to be facing fore-
closure than whites. . . . As a result of the disproportionate
number of foreclosures borne by African Americans and
Latinos, the 'spillover' costs, in the form of depreciated
home values, increased crime rates, and community blight,
are likely to hit communities of color particularly hard."[13]

Ryan Bowers cofounded an organization applying shareholder activism strategies to municipal bonds.
Because investment in municipal bonds is a tax-saving
strategy, it's usually wealthy people who invest in them.
"In a state like, let's say, Alabama," Ryan tells me, "most
of the bond investors are mostly old, white, rich men.
Municipal bonds are fifteen to twenty percent of their
total portfolio. They refuse to invest, for example, in historically Black colleges and universities." The same thing

happens in border towns, he says. "Particularly in Texas or other border states, they don't want to invest in the municipal bonds of places that serve a lot of immigrants or potentially undocumented immigrants." As a result of this, "these municipalities have to pay more when they go to the bond market. It takes a longer time for them to find investors, and those bonds sit in the inventory of their brokers longer. It's totally unfair. There's no real laws or framework protecting against that."[14]

Municipal bonds for Native tribal governments are the most restricted, in what Ryan calls an "overseer relationship" with the federal government. When tribes want to pave roads, build housing, or launch other economic development projects, they are not simply permitted to issue bonds for that work, as is any non-Native municipality in the country. They have to get permission from the feds. According to Ryan, historically Black colleges and universities "are experiencing redlining in the municipal bond market, but tribal colleges don't even have municipal bonds. There's no investment going into them."

Ryan transitions from there to enlightening me about the role of ratings agencies. They define risk and do underwriting by looking at a city's general fund balance, the debt service coverage ratio.

> People talk about philanthropy being like a shadow government. Well, the ratings agencies are really the shadow. They have so much power over the cost of capital for a city. They look at the percentage of nonwhite people in the community; for them, that is an indicator of more people on welfare and people who are going to have antisocial behavior and increase your costs. The Fair

Lending Act and other civil rights legislation that protects lenders hasn't really made it to the municipal finance market yet.

Ryan and his colleagues worked in Ferguson, Missouri, in 2014, after the police murdered Michael Brown, a Black teenager, which led to protests and a militarized response from the police.

Essentially the credit ratings agencies, the municipal credit ratings agencies, annuities, and Standard and Poor's, they ended up downgrading Ferguson's bonds rating, saying they're not going to be able to service their debt and or honor these new obligations. Once Ferguson's bond rating got downgraded, the cost of borrowing was going to go through the roof for the next ten years. Everything was going to cost more—more in interest, more in underwriting fees. They were actually making the city pay for it.

Across the board, among all institutions of finance and wealth, the fundamental dynamic is that control remains in the hands of the old boys' network. Mostly white saviors and experts use hoarded wealth to dominate and control—obviously or subtly—the seekers and recipients of those funds. Our means and mechanisms perpetuate the very problems in the world we claim to wish to solve.

CHAPTER FIVE

The Overseers

What happens when the power and privilege conferred by access to money lead to the savior complex and destructive colonial-style leadership

After several years at Kate B. Reynolds, managing a sizable high-impact portfolio that began to receive some national attention in the field, I was invited to serve on the boards of several organizations. I won some awards and fellowships. The most prestigious came from Grantmakers in Health, which selected me to be among the very first class of Terrance Keenan Institute fellows. Terrance Keenan, affectionately known as Terry, had been one of the first staff members at the Robert Wood Johnson Foundation, a health-focused powerhouse. In his monograph on philanthropy, *The Promise at Hand*, he wrote, "A great foundation is informed and animated by moral purpose. . . . A great foundation walks humbly with its grantees—it acknowledges that their success is the instrument of its own success."[1] Terry's obituary on March 7, 2009, in the *New York Times* noted, "Terry set the standard for creativity, caring and vision in philanthropy. What made

Terry so special is that he never lost sight of the people we are trying to help. His modus operandi was to always remember that the Foundation represents a public trust."[2]

The fellowship was a yearlong program focused on leadership development. We were the cream of the crop in health philanthropy, folks who were positioned to move into executive positions in the next three to five years. Everything was going so well for me.

It was at this point that I started getting the sense that some did not like the attention that I was receiving.

One day my boss came into my office and told me, "The way that you're working is making the other program officers feel bad. They've been coming to me saying you're on all these boards, and you're looked at as a leader. They're not on boards. I just think that maybe you shouldn't be on boards." Her stance was that all program officers should be the same and that the experience from the communities' perspective should be consistency—like the service you get from McDonald's.

I was very close with two of the other program officers, both of whom were white women and older than I. We had lunch together every day. We talked about everything. We hung out outside work and are still friends to this day. So, directly after my boss's comment, during lunch, I asked them outright, "Am I making y'all feel bad?"

"We have no idea what you're talking about," they protested. "We wouldn't say that. We're so proud of your leadership."

I was utterly confused. My boss had always been my mentor. I was *her person*—the first staff member she had personally hired. We'd made a great team: I implemented her strategies; I was her agent of change.

Serving on boards was a professional development opportunity that raised not only my profile but also the foundation's. And I wasn't neglecting my work at KBR; I was as much of an overachiever as I had been the day I'd arrived, six years prior.

I attempted to raise the issue with her, to tell her I'd checked in with the other program officers and discovered they had no objections, but she interpreted this as insubordination. She told me I needed to work on my ability to receive feedback.

Despite the fact that it made no sense, I was forced to resign from all my board positions. I began to feel like I was being told to keep my head down. I felt silenced.

Then, at a meeting in front of our entire board of directors, she remarked—offhand, jokingly, but one of those jokes with a razor-sharp, serious edge under it—"Edgar, you are getting too big for your britches!"

For those of you needing a translation of this Southern idiom, this statement is a phrase of ridicule used as far back as the sixteenth century, meaning that my assumed position or sense of importance was exaggerated or larger than the position I'd been granted. The phrase is meant to diminish, oppress, or even threaten someone who may be esteeming himself too highly. It insinuates the need for an adjustment.

Not long after, she called me into her office and asked, "Edgar, where do you want to be in five years?"

"Well, I think I want to be the CEO of a foundation one day."

She nodded. "I thought so." And then she said, "I want to help you. Let's figure out a plan. You're too big for KBR. You should be at Ford, Kellogg, somewhere. Let's get you out of here and to positions that are going to get you where you need to go."

I was so grateful. She was very well connected, a former executive coach. We set my departure date as one year from that meeting and I began applying for jobs—program officer positions at bigger foundations, or vice president positions, one step up from where I was. Often we'd do a mock interview together before, to prepare me for the interviews.

Still, I didn't get any job offers.

During this time, KBR held a capacity-building training for our grantees, way out in the far east side of the state. We brought in a nationally known consultant to lead it. He was very well regarded and professional. After the training, as I was driving him to the airport, he told me he had heard I was leaving the foundation.

"This is really uncomfortable for me to say," he said, "but I just feel like I need to tell you this. I think that you're trusting the wrong people with your career. I can't say too much, but I think you should just start keeping things to yourself and not telling people."

What the heck was he talking about? Who was he talking to? What was happening?

I was thoroughly confused by this conversation, and on the long drive back to Winston-Salem, I decided to call my mentor, who worked at the University of North Carolina at Chapel Hill. I had recently applied for a director-level position at the school. I was in the final running for the job and was excited about the opportunity.

He answered his phone on the first ring. "Where are you right now?"

I told him the exit I'd just passed.

"Oh my God, take the next exit." It was eerie, almost supernatural, that we were in the same place, both so far from home, at the same moment. I pulled off at the following exit and we followed each other into a McDonald's parking lot. We went in, ordered some drinks, and sat down.

"I need to talk with you about something," he began. "Know I did not want to tell you this. This is terrible, but

I feel like there's a reason you called me, and why we were both right here. I have to tell you this. I know you're in an extremely competitive position for the job at UNC. Someone from the foundation called me."

Other than me, he didn't even know folks at the foundation well—definitely not well enough to receive this kind of call. And no one there knew that he and I knew each other, that we were in fact very close.

"They called me and said, 'Look, I need to tell you some stuff about Edgar. Y'all would be making a huge mistake if you hired him.'"

He went on, describing how they had made me out to be a severely problematic person, practically a monster.

I told him that made no sense at all, that the leadership of the foundation had literally been coaching me through the job search process. Why would anyone say awful things about me behind my back?

"You have got to shut it down."

I literally wept as I drove back to Winston-Salem. Beyond the job thing, I was personally devastated.

I didn't know how to handle it. My future was in the hands of the foundation. KBR gave a lot of money to everyone, including UNC. Even if people didn't believe what was said about me, no one in the state was going to endanger their relationship with the foundation by hiring me. The evaporation of trust was torturous, because I loved my work at the foundation and loved and respected the leadership. I didn't want to say anything bad about it or anything bad about the leadership. I had understood that it was my time to go, and I was leaving, but could I just land a new job first? I mean, I had a mortgage, thanks to Oprah. Ultimately, I had to keep my job search process a secret. I'd just give vague updates when asked.

I faced the threat of going back into poverty. I couldn't
get a job. I was terrified that my life was going to fall apart.
I became physically ill, highly anxious, and unable to eat. I
developed irritable bowel syndrome. My hair started falling
out, a stress-related condition called alopecia. I had to go
into therapy. I went to pastoral counseling. I asked people
who prayed seriously to pray for me. In the end, I moved
my departure date up and left the foundation early, without
even having a job lined up. I just knew that I had to get out
of there.

Eating Our Own

In telling you my story, I left out something about my boss
at KBR: she is African American. While I was living through
it, this fact made the situation all the more heartbreaking,
but in retrospect, it's also allowed me to find compassion
and forgiveness. She was the first woman ever to hold that
leadership position at KBR; she also was the first Black
person to do so. As a Black woman, she took it upon herself to challenge the status quo of the foundation and its
good old boys board and community network. I can't fully
imagine what kind of pressure she was under or how she
may have suffered. I can imagine how she may have felt
when I began to get more attention and to shine brighter.
When I told her that my aspiration was to become the head
of a foundation myself, that could have been the final straw.
Maybe my ambition was too unbridled.

Over the years, I've seen really terrible behavior between
people of color within philanthropy, I believe because the
space for us feels so limited. Inside these privileged, powerful places that are almost entirely white, occasionally a
"designated space" opens up for you as a person of color,

a token. Quite possibly you've never had access to power, and all of a sudden, you're going to these fancy dinners and having meetings with CEOs and mayors. There is a sense of specialness and scarcity, that there's only a few of us who get in the door, and so you want to hold on to your spot and to the little bit of power and privilege that you have. All of a sudden there's another person of color. You almost can't help being afraid that person might take it all away from you. It can make us behave terribly toward one another. Some of my friends call this the "shiny new penny syndrome."

While I had hoped that she and other leaders would celebrate my accomplishments as a Southern Native American working in institutional philanthropy, I have had to push through diminishment and oppression at every turn of my professional life for the past decade—usually from leaders from whom I sought support and guidance.

Later, after a break from philanthropy following my departure from KBR, I heard about an interesting opportunity at a foundation in Seattle. It was about as far in the opposite direction as I could go and still be in the field of philanthropy. I don't mean geographically, although that was also true. Unlike the Southern tobacco dynasty rooted in slavery, the money behind this new foundation came from a classic entrepreneurial American rags-to-riches story.

In 1899, in Seattle, 11-year-old Jim Casey had to drop out of school to find work because of his father's failing health. Jim was the eldest of the four Casey kids. He started out as a delivery boy for a department store, earning $2.50 per month. When he was 19, he borrowed $100 to cofound a small messenger service with a buddy. "It consisted of six messengers, two bicycles, and a telephone, operating from a 6-by-17-foot basement of a saloon." It was the Little

Engine That Could, and it grew and it grew until it became the world's largest package delivery company, UPS. Several foundations focused on the well-being of families and children were created with the resulting wealth.[3]

In contrast to KBR, this foundation operates nationwide, espousing some of the most explicitly progressive values you can find in philanthropy. They cite transparency and accountability, equity, mutual trust and respect, and antiracism among their guiding values. Their grantees are organizations doing some of the smartest, most innovative work to address the root causes of poverty, inequality, and discrimination.

And yet . . . !

In this new foundation, I experienced what I perceived to be another case of internalized oppression, far more nefarious than my experience at KBR. Even today, having left there and moved on to greener pastures, I still share the traumatic experiences of many staff who worked at that institution and that have since been chronicled in the media. This is what the power of the overseer can do. Have you seen Miranda Priestly in *The Devil Wears Prada*? Yeah.

Here, alliances had sprung up between the grantees themselves and the grantmaking staff as the controlling, overseer-type behavior was well known and had been experienced by many. The grantees had actually learned to look out for the staff, to support them, to say whatever they needed to say to keep their program officers in good favor, thereby protecting their internal ally for future funding. Most of the grantees had learned the art of flattering my boss in order to keep the checks coming, because she had the power to approve all grants—every penny. Organizations were added and removed from the docket with no explanation, leaving us program officers to come up with some halfway believable reason. The act of funding so many stellar organizations had created delusions of grandeur and a definite entitlement in the foundation's leadership, which by the end of my tenure was pursuing its own political organization, with the idea of ultimately becoming the largest organization in America to fight on behalf of poor families. Everyone was terrified to tell the empress that she had no clothes, for fear of retaliation that could diminish funding to the grantees.

The staff was kept at a distance in order to control the narrative with the board. It wouldn't do for them to question the leadership's judgments about the staff and our work, or decisions about firing and restructuring. Many dozens of people had come and gone through this foundation, and it was less than a decade old. Tragically, the leadership style absolutely embodied the mantra of colonizers: "Divide, control, [and above all] exploit."

I had thought the leadership at KBR was a tragic example of internalized oppression, but this place would take it to a whole other level, where the hunger for power seemed to have no limits. And I am far from alone in having had these kinds of terrible experiences with the very people I would most have hoped to be supported by.

~~~~

A year after the first Terry Keenan fellowship ended, all of us who had been in that first class convened to check in and catch up with each other. When I started counting the changes, something like 23 percent of us no longer worked in philanthropy. Why were 23 percent of the field's supposed brightest stars no longer working in philanthropy?

When I asked the fellows why they had left, people had their own camera-ready responses, things like "I wanted a more authentic relationship with community" or "I just felt like it was the time for a transition for me." I dug deeper, and I started calling people one-on-one, and I shared my story. What I found out was that almost every single person had the same story.

We lacked role models and mentors, people who looked like us. We lacked access to informal networks that translated to power. We were limited by stereotypes and preconceptions of our aptitudes and cutting edges. We were pushed out because we were not status quo. We were pushed out because we were asking the hard questions about "underserved populations" (code for "Black and brown folks"). We were pushed out when the leadership, be it boards or bosses, could not handle our gifts and made us miserable until we left. We were treated as disposable. We were treated with no sense of dignity.

One of the darkest, most insidious results of the trauma of racism and colonization is internalized oppression. Here we all are, Natives and people of color and white people, living together inside a complex global system that has normalized treating certain kinds of people as less than worthy, even questioning their right to exist—from immigrants to Indigenous, from people with disabilities to people of color, from women and girls to queer folk to people holding low-status jobs. When you live inside a system like this, breathing the air, drinking the water, watching the television, it is beyond easy to absorb the cultural attitudes, myths, and stereotypes; in fact, it's almost a given that you'll be affected by it and infected by it. Internalized oppression involves consciously or unconsciously adopting the mindset of the exploiter, the oppressor, the hater.

Because it's generally not safe to lash out against the actual perpetrators, this kind of behavior plays out where it is "safe," which, tragically, means turning this mindset toward yourself or toward members of your own group—especially those over whom you have some degree of control. You perpetuate the abusive treatment that you received at the hands of those who diminished, exploited, and abused you. You turn it against your already wounded self and your fellow wounded. Internalized oppression is heartbreaking.

With yourself, internalized oppression may manifest as feelings of inferiority, inadequacy, self-hatred, self-invalidation, self-doubt, isolation, fear, powerlessness, and despair. You might drive yourself into the ground in a quest for perfection and acceptance—or the opposite: you might throw in the towel and stop showing up for school or for work. You might develop compulsive behaviors, eating disorders, addictions. You might walk around loudly protesting that exploitation and oppression of people like yourself is a total myth. You might get stuck in one abusive relationship after another. You might suffer from depression, or have intense, disruptive outbursts of bitterness or anger. All of these behaviors map onto internalized oppression.

Around others, it may look like name-calling, stereotyping, or character assassination. You might be rude or dismissive when members of your group dress in a traditional way or otherwise take steps to connect to their heritage. You might psychologically abuse people from your community who have lower-status jobs than you in your workplace. You might gossip, backstab, blame.

Internalized oppression can mean we don't respect ourselves, and we cover it with self-righteousness. We toughen our children up and focus on their flaws with the intention of making them invincible. We project our negativity and feelings of powerlessness on our own leaders, who make easy targets. We complain rather than taking responsibility for making things better.

The Savior Dynamic

When I speak to young professionals in philanthropy and finance now, I always tell them, "You have to be careful about the Whitney Houston–Bobby Brown syndrome." When Whitney was married to Bobby Brown, anytime she was in public with him, she declared him the greatest entertainer of all time, with a shout and a wave of the hand. It was like she had to diminish herself and publicly announce that he was a bigger star than she was, in order to thrive in that relationship. You can be a leader in the community and outside the institution, where you can shine bright as a diamond, but you can't steal the spotlight of someone else at your organization who has more power than you—especially if they're occupying one of the few coveted spots for token minorities.

Because of the power associated with controlling wealth, leaders in institutions of philanthropy and finance are some of worst perpetrators of the savior dynamic. Despite all their talk of wanting to help, reform, even revolutionize the world, saviors won't touch the underlying system of privilege and power because that's what grants them their status and position in the world. In the end, saviors don't heal anything. The savior complex often goes hand in hand with white supremacy. Not all saviors are white; some are people of color and Indigenous people who have been infected by the power dynamic of colonization and internalized oppression.

Here's the thing about saviors: no matter how much they think the victim may need their help, rescuing someone can only reinforce their victimhood. There's a theory from psychology around this dynamic called the drama triangle. It states that there are three roles in abusive or oppressive situations: perpetrator, victim, and savior. Victims hurt, perpetrators inflict the hurt, and saviors relieve or remove the hurt. These three interlocking roles work together to create cycles of hurt, blame, and guilt that continue endlessly unless we awaken to them.

The key to escaping the drama triangle dynamic is to shift from looking for affirmation and purpose externally, outside oneself, from others. Everyone must take full responsibility for her/himself and learn to cultivate purpose and worth internally, without needing the other players in the power dynamic. When we have transcended the triangle, we embody the "both/and" of the famous quote from Dr. Martin Luther King Jr.: "Power without love is reckless and abusive, and love without power is sentimental and anemic. Power at its best is love implementing the demands of justice, and justice at its best is love correcting everything that stands against love."[4]

Internalized oppression limits us just as much as the oppression coming from someone else. It limits the thoughts we can think, the dreams we can dream, the actions we can take, the futures we can create. It is an aspect of trauma from which we must heal, in order to stop the cycles of division, exploitation, and hurt.

CHAPTER SIX

Freedom

How our focus on individual leaders is also a reflection of the colonizer virus

Around the time I left KBR, I got my Indian name. I wish I could tell you a romantic story about a vision quest where I became a man after spending a month building my own shelter, sleeping under the stars, foraging and nearly starving, and having hallucinogenic experiences that revealed the true nature of things. But that's not how it happened.

No, it was in a beige conference room at the Marriott in Denver. I had found a job, finally, in the direct aftermath of KBR, and was running the North Carolina American Indian Health Board, an organization that represented the six tribes around the state, working toward improved health in our communities, and the National Indian Health Board conference was taking place in Denver. At the conference was a sign-up sheet to meet with an Ojibwe medicine man.

Obviously, I signed up.

There was a line of people waiting their turn to go into the room and have a session with him, and I was nervous.

In my church, growing up, this kind of thing—shamans and the like—would have been condemned as heresy.

"What's going to happen in there?" I asked the woman waiting in line in front of me. I felt like I was on my way to see the Great and Powerful Oz.

She looked at me doubtfully and asked, "Do you have tobacco to give him?"

Um. I don't carry around tobacco with me. "Is that what they like?" I asked.

"You have to take a gift!" she said, shocked at my ignorance. She broke off a bit of hers and gave it to me.

I went in, holding the tobacco out in front of me. The medicine man nodded at his assistant to take it from me, and gestured for me to sit down. We sat in generic hotel chairs across from each other at a generic hotel table. He was wearing something vaguely ceremonial but not extravagant. I was wearing my usual colonized attire: as nice a suit as I could afford.

He stared at me for a moment. I felt very uncomfortable, skeptical but hopeful at the same time.

He asked me why I'd come. The truth was someone had suggested that if I were lucky, he might give me an Indian name, even though it's pretty unusual for someone from another tribe to give you a name. There are different traditions around naming. My tribe does not have a naming ceremony. You are just who you are, whatever your mama names you. I felt I'd be more legit with a real Indian name, but of course I wasn't going to express that to the medicine man.

So I said, "I'm part of this organization, trying to help my community. I'm trying to get reconnected to my culture because I did not grow up in traditional Native ways. I just want to open my mind to all of this, so that I can be in a better position to help my community back in North Carolina." I was babbling a bit.

"The ancestors are happy that you're here," he said.

What? My colonized mind kicked in, wondering if this dude was totally making stuff up. At the same time, I thought I might burst into tears.

He talked about the colors he saw coming from me. His eyes flickered around the room as he spoke, and suddenly he flinched and practically ducked: the ancestors and spirits were flying around the room, he told me.

Okay, this was definitely ridiculous. Wasn't it? I had no idea. I wanted to scream and run out of the room, but I couldn't move. I was transfixed. And then he said it: "I want to give you an Indian name."

My moment had arrived. My prayers had been granted.

Niigaanii Beneshi.

It's in Ojibwe, from northern Minnesota.

"It means 'Leading Bird,'" he added, sparing me from having to find someone who speaks Ojibwe to translate it for me. "When birds are flying in the V formation, there's a bird that's leading the formation. That's you."

I thanked him and floated out of the room, feeling all spiritual and mysterious after the experience. Niigaanii Beneshi. Leading Bird.

~~~

After I left him, I researched the qualities of migratory birds. It turns out migration is no party. More birds die during migration than at any other time, from dehydration, starvation, or sheer exhaustion. When birds fly together, they cut the wind for each other—all except for the one at the front. That one has to bear the full force of the wind.

That one has to stick his nose out. That one has to lead the way forward despite the discomfort.

At the same time, one of the great lessons of migrating birds is that they take turns occupying that tough position at the front, which allows for greater resilience for the whole group. By working together, a flock of birds is greater than the sum of its parts. In her book *Emergent Strategy*, adrienne maree brown writes about what we can learn from flocks of birds:

> There is a right relationship, a right distance between them—too close and they crash, too far away and they can't feel the micro-adaptations of the other bodies. Each creature is shifting direction, speed, and proximity based on the information of the other creatures' bodies.

> There is a deep trust in this: to lift because the birds around you are lifting, to live based on your collective real-time adaptations. In this way thousands of birds or fish or bees can move together, each empowered with basic rules and a vision to live. Imagine our movements cultivating this type of trust and depth with each other, having strategic flocking in our playbooks.

> Adaptation reduces exhaustion. No one bears the burden alone of figuring out the next move and muscling towards it. There is an efficiency at play—is something not working? Stop. Change. If something is working, keep doing it—learning and innovating as you go.[1]

The lesson is that thriving is not actually about the leader; it's about the whole flock. Everyone has the potential to lead, and leadership is about listening and being attuned to everyone else. It's about flexibility. It's about humility. It's about trust. It's about having fun along the way. It is more about holding space for others' brilliance than being the sole source of answers, more about flexible shape-shifting to meet the oncoming challenges than holding fast to a five-year strategic plan.

I am frequently asked what decolonized leadership looks like. Compassionate, empathetic, vulnerable leaders? Servant leaders? Leaders who listen? Yes, and it's not about the individual. We have to shift from our obsession with individual leaders to a focus on organizational design, which tends to be taken for granted and invisible in most of our institutions.

Fortunately, conversations about new kinds of organizational design have been exploding recently. There's a sea change happening, moving us away from the colonized hierarchical pyramid structure, with its command-and-control leadership, to a realization of how everyone has leadership potential. Businesses have been at the forefront of experimenting with organizational models that transcend the colonized mindset of division, control, and exploitation; now it's time for the fields of philanthropy and finance to follow their lead, in order to heal divides and restore balance.

~~~

The day after I received my name, the Native health conference ended. As I was heading to my gate at the Denver airport, I saw the medicine man wearing a T-shirt and jeans, eating at TGI Fridays. That's the modern Native American existence for you. Natives can be both denim-wearing, television-watching, fast-food-eating people, on the one hand, and people who honor the ancestors, participate in ceremonial rituals, and prepare traditional feasts, on the other.

I was reminded of an observation from my mentor, a Lumbee elder named Donna Chavis, who worked in institutional philanthropy before me, one of the very first Native women to do so. She had been telling stories about her grandfather, "a Bible-thumping Baptist preacher. His way of being was not just Christian; it was a blend, because he was a traditional healer too. He made the connection." As I've mentioned, the contemporary Lumbee identity inevitably includes faith in Christianity, a result of the fact that we were colonized 500-some years ago.

"Blending Native tradition with Christianity made it possible to move through both worlds. There was not a rejection—it was not either/or—it was *both/and*. The *both/and* mindset influenced just about everything in the way I was raised within our clan. I think the word 'mutual' captures it," said Donna. "'Mutual' means that both sides have something to offer, and that's what's true."[2]

When the both/and disappears and Indigenous people have to choose either the colonizers' way or the traditional way, and reject the other way, including whatever good might exist within it, they tend to be much less resilient. There are studies on alcoholism among Natives, Donna told me, that show that the Indians with the highest chance of becoming alcoholics are the ones on either end of the spectrum—those who completely adopt the ways of the colonizers and those who completely reject them. "It was those who learned *not only* how to respect and live within their culture *but also* to navigate the world outside their culture who wound up having the lower risk of alcoholism," she told me.

Being Native means living in the complex space where worlds meet. Members of Native American tribes literally hold dual nationalities, first as citizens of their Native nation and second as citizens of the United States. Today, in our everyday lives, we do not dress like Natives portrayed in movies like *Dances with Wolves*. We blend in; we're wearing jeans (or the latest B.Yellowtail fashions) and jet-setting. We're getting degrees in law and Western medicine. At the same time, we've still got a connection to the land on which we've always lived, to the places where our ancestors are buried, to our songs and our medicine.

"Integration means we can lift up what we have. At the same time, we bring in what is needed," as Donna says. Accepting the both/and nature of things was key to Indigenous survival against all odds.

By the time I left KBR I was fairly thoroughly colonized, after years of church, mainstream schooling and higher education, and then the oh-so-white experience of the foundation built with tobacco money. It's no coincidence that it was at this point in my story that I really began the process of becoming more curious about my Native heritage and connecting with Indigenous traditions. For modern Natives, the process of decolonization often looks like this, an exploration and embrace of traditional rituals and practices from which one has become disconnected.

"The essence of trauma is disconnection from ourselves," says Gabor Maté, a Hungarian-born doctor who is one of the world's top experts on trauma. "Trauma is not terrible things that happen from the other side—those are *traumatic*. But the trauma is that very separation from the body and emotions. So, the real question is, 'How did we get separated and how do we reconnect?' Because that's our true nature—our true nature is to be connected."[3]

Becoming reconnected—overcoming the mindset of separation—is how humans heal from trauma. Reconnecting can mean remembering traditions and honoring our community's wisdom. It can mean researching our family history and find-ing out how our wealth was generated. It will probably mean remembering and reexperiencing painful events. I know this was the case for me. There's so much that I had pushed out of my memory, that I had wanted to forget.

Reconnecting might mean having vulnerable, difficult, awkward conversations with people who are harmed by the system from which we benefit. It may entail forgiveness of those who have harmed us. It means recognizing that we are part of something greater, that we belong together, that we are all in this thing called life together. This is all part of the path to freedom, to really restoring balance in our lives and in the world.

But—for me at least—it's not simply just a full return to the ancient ways; it's the both/and integration. I have no intention of acquiring traditional skills like hunting and skinning game or building canoes or shelters by hand. I intend to keep working with money, guiding people to think about it as medicine, as a tool of decolonizing and healing. I am keeping my tailored suits (tailored in my head, at least!) and my Brooklyn apartment. As they say about relationship status: *It's complicated.*

I firmly believe that integrating my Native heritage has contributed to my resilience as I have gone on to new roles within philanthropy and to encounter even greater chal-lenges. As I've faced off with more overseers, saviors, and my own internalized oppression, I've been able to call upon the aspects of myself that are Lumbee, that are the Leading Bird.

As humanity faces all kinds of challenges that have come from the separation worldview—the devastation of the planet, the hate and fear among different religions and races and political ideologies—cultivating integration will be key to healing and saving all of us, and to restoring bal-ance to the world.

PART TWO

Being a Healer

I didn't think of myself as a healer before writing this book. If I was anything, I was a *survivor*. I'd survived the trauma of growing up poor and Native American. I'd survived the pain of betrayals and disillusionment as a young professional of color in a white-dominated sector. For so long, I was singing "I Will Survive" along with Gloria Gaynor, at the top of my lungs.

As I started the process of writing, I began thinking of myself as a *whistle-blower*. I set out to write about my experiences and the experiences of people like me, people of color and Indigenous people working inside ivory tower institutions that reflect the dynamics of the colonizer virus. I wanted to make people like me feel seen and heard, validated and witnessed. So many folks out there had been asking themselves *Am I crazy or are they crazy?* They'd been stuck in the gaslighting of institutional culture. They'd been working in difficult situations with complicated power dynamics. They were afraid to speak up, and so they'd just been suppressing all those feelings—the way I had, myself, until it made me sick. I wanted to call out all those who had made us suffer. I wasn't above shaming the most callous of them.

What I didn't anticipate was that the process of writing and sharing the book would not just heal me but also transform me into someone regarded as a *healer*. The journey took me into dark places in myself, unearthing painful things I'd repressed and had to grieve; and then joyously connected me with my Indigenous roots and the elders in my community. And on the other side of that, I somehow had become a . . . healer.

At first it was awkward. A little bit of the imposter syndrome crept in. I blushed when someone introducing me at an event referred to me as a healer. I mean, was I old enough to be considered a healer? Should I be dressing differently—maybe some ceremonial regalia like the medicine man who had given me my Native name? And could I keep making references to pop culture? Would I have to act serious all the time? Should I carry around sage or anointing oil?

It turned out I didn't have to wear anything special. It turned out that humor, even pop culture references, sometimes helped me connect with someone more than a quote from a philosopher or a passage from the Bible ever would have—and to be a healer, you have to be able to connect.

It turned out I didn't need to alter myself in any way; I just needed to show up and be myself. For a lot of us, it is actually harder than it sounds to stay true to yourself, to maintain integrity, in a world where so many adopt the ways of the colonizer in order to wield influence. Sometimes people talk about integrity like it means the same thing as honesty, and of course that's part of it, the integrity of your word. But having integrity is more than that. It's literally about keeping the shape of your whole self intact. In my case, in the worlds in which I travel, staying authentic is often a vulnerable thing to do.

And "showing up" doesn't just mean walking into the room. It means having your heart in the space, too. It means being present. It means listening deeply, openly, without filters.

It turned out that being a healer didn't mean I had to be perfect.

There is a responsibility involved in being a healer, of course, but it's actually not to heal people. The power to heal is something that each one of us has access to inside ourselves, and what a healer does is to remind us of that power, or to unlock something so we can connect to that power. Healing happens through learning about ourselves, forgiving ourselves, and loving ourselves. Healers can hold up a mirror to others, but we can't do the healing for them.

Despite my initial resistance, I've embraced the identity of healer. It is a powerful place to stand, with magic in it.

And because of my own transformative experience, I believe we all have the potential to be healers. Listen up, though, because there is a catch! Before becoming a healer of others, we must first heal ourselves. People who haven't healed themselves first may perpetuate dysfunctional dynamics, like the internalized oppression and other cycles of trauma described in the first part of the book. If you feel like this may be true for you, you may have to work through the Seven Steps to Healing in part 3 of this book first. That journey might be difficult, as mine was, but there is unexplainable joy in emerging on the other side and becoming an effective healer. And when we see ourselves as healers, we stand to make a deeper impact upon the world. Just as many kinds of things and events can serve as medicine, there are almost infinite opportunities for us to serve as healers.

CHAPTER SEVEN

Medicine
Beyond Money

What's your medicine? How will you recognize an opportunity to be a healer? After the release of the first edition of *Decolonizing Wealth*, I got to meet and dialogue with all kinds of people. Like ripples extending out over the surface of the water, the conversations went further than the scope of the book, to places I had not expected. People shared how they suddenly had recognized the colonizer dynamics of *divide, control, exploit* in everything from the daily news to their personal relationships, from their kids' school curriculum to the shows they were bingeing on Netflix. What became clear is that the colonizer virus is present pretty much everywhere. While on the one hand that's disheartening and uncomfortable to see, on the other hand, it means that there are opportunities for the work of decolonization and healing in almost every workplace and sector, even inside relationships and families. Healing in this wider sense means sharing, redistributing, or even outright giving back resources.

As I share some stories of people I've met who have told me about the work that the book has inspired them to do, I invite you to reflect on what you might have access to beyond money, such as other kinds of resources, skills, opportunities, or wealth. And I invite you to think creatively about how you could use them to advance healing.

In 2020, Camille Kalama, an Indigenous woman living on the Big Island of Hawaii, shared her story with me. Her path had been somewhat like mine. She had attended ivory tower institutions to get her degrees, earning a doctorate in law. After graduating from law school, she worked for the Hawaii Supreme Court, and then she became the staff attorney of the Native Hawaiian Legal Corporation. It was purposeful work, resolving conflicts over land rights and protecting Native rights, and Camille felt fulfilled, until one day the mountain called to her—Maunakea.

Indigenous Hawaiians consider Maunakea the meeting point of Earth Mother and Sky Father. For a decade Native Hawaiians have been protesting plans to build the Thirty Meter Telescope (TMT) on Maunakea, as it would disrupt the extremely fragile ecosystem and desecrate sacred cultural sites, including burial sites. If built, it would be the largest telescope in the Northern Hemisphere, reaching 180 feet, or more than 18 stories high, at its tallest point.

Tragically, the TMT project's biggest funder is a philanthropic institution, the Gordon and Betty Moore Foundation, which has simultaneously invested more than $350 million in conservation efforts for Indigenous lands in the Andean Amazon and supports communities in Alaska and British Colombia that rely on wild salmon. The foundation is a classic example of causing the problems with one hand that it is attempting to solve with the other hand. It's an example of being so bound in a construct of superiority that one can't even understand what's at stake and how this is hurting the planet and oneself.

When the mountain protectors contacted the foundation and requested it withdraw its funding or make funding of the telescope conditional on it being built on another site (a site in Spain has been identified as a viable alternative), the request was denied. Betty Moore allegedly referred to Maunakea as "just a pile of rocks."

The company behind TMT's construction claims they've gone through all the necessary legal and environmental reviews, that its construction will create jobs, and that because the telescope's purpose is scientific, it's neutral and won't have an impact on the environment.

"Our people know better," Camille says. "We know that money is fleeting and the land is here forever. We've been there, done that, and we also know that these jobs go to other people from outside, and they're short-term jobs only."

The TMT is just the latest in a long line of abuse and violence against the peaceful Native people of Hawaii, a continuum of disregard, disrespect, and dehumanization, prioritizing economic interests ahead of community interests. For the Natives, it's about the misuse of occupied Hawaiian national lands, which are supposed to be held in trust by the State of Hawaii, similar to treaty lands in the continental United States. The movement to regain control of Native lands and resources has been going on since the 1970s, beginning with reclaiming the Hawaiian language and cultural practices, which had been largely condemned and even outlawed after Hawaii was seized by the United States in 1893.

Despite the best efforts of Native Hawaiian activists for more than a decade, in July 2019, the governor of Hawaii announced that the construction of the TMT was starting. The mountain was going to go the way of all the other broken treaties and shattered promises made to Natives.

At that point, the activists' strategy shifted to nonviolent direct action, physically occupying Maunakea and creating a *pu'uhonua* (traditional sanctuary) space with the sanctification of a kahuna (medicine man), which traditionally would protect anyone inside its boundaries. In this refuge, they set up a camp like the one at Standing Rock. From there, they held the line against moneyed interests, arrests by the police, even crackdowns by the National Guard. The number of people at the camp grew from 33 on the first day to approximately 2,000 by the end of the first week.

Camille was part of the organizing team that planned the occupation. "After the first three weeks up on the mountain, I called my job and said 'Hey, I can't come back.' I decided I was going to resign." She told me:

> If you could imagine one point for your people that was the most important, this is it, and we are committed. We've been here for generations, for hundreds of years protecting this place, and we plan to be here for hundreds more. So if you think your fifty-year project is going to overwhelm us, you're wrong. We are raising the next generations to understand how to do what we're doing, and they are just as, if not more, committed than any of us.

I was struck by Camille's immediate recognition of the call, and her fierce resolve in quitting her job. She clearly heard the medicine that was reaching out to her and inviting her to step into a new, different role as a healer. Remember: you don't choose the medicine; you stay open and let the medicine choose you.

And once one person steps up to do healing work, it often attracts more healing. I actually first heard about

Maunakea at a funders' conference in October 2019, where I was supposed to give the closing keynote. But the person who spoke before me was Andre Perez of the Hawai'i Unity & Liberation Institute, one of the organizations that had been coordinating the protection of the mountain. Andre had flown straight from the camp to the conference in Chicago. I was so moved by his passion that when it was my turn to speak, I just balled up my notes and threw them away and turned to the audience of funders in the room. "We need to respond to this right now. This man has just poured out his heart and is literally putting his life in danger for our future. We are funders—we should be responding right now to support this." I'm proud to say there were folks in that room, including the Ford Foundation, who just wrote a check, no application required, no runaround—just "untethered funding," as I call it. We raised $40,000 in a matter of moments.

This is how healing can snowball, attracting more medicine, with the passion of one healer irresistibly attracting medicine from others.

~~~

Are you able to sense more opportunities in your own life? As I've said, many kinds of things can serve as medicine.

For example, there were two particular people in Hollywood who got fired up about the first edition of this book: Dawn-Lyen Gardner, the star of the family drama *Queen Sugar*; and the actor Matt McGorry, best known for his roles in *Orange Is the New Black* and *How to Get Away with Murder*. And let me tell you, fame is wealth. Whether you're an Instagram influencer, a big deal on Broadway, or a Hollywood star, just having the prestige and the attention of a lot of followers is a powerful resource. At the events I did together with Dawn-Lyen and Matt, we discussed who "has the microphone" and what kind of opportunity and responsibility comes with that power.

Dawn-Lyen was my featured guest at our Decolonizing Wealth event in New Orleans, and she amplified both it and my work across all her platforms, getting people all over the country tuning into our conversation about decolonization. She actively uses her platform to advocate for racial justice, voting, and other issues. Matt is a voracious reader of books about feminism and racial justice. He highlights them and shares those passages on his Instagram. Both those actions are easy ways to leverage celebrity status. You can do a lot of healing in the world when you have that many people following you and looking up to you.

Matt actually cofounded an organization called Inspire Justice with JLove Calderón, a white activist and creator, who developed a curriculum to influence the entertainment industry on issues of racial justice. They've offered trainings to casts and crews and advised Hollywood executives on what it looks like to use that platform to further justice. There are questions of who gets the chance to direct, who gets cast, whose story is depicted, all of which have powerful implications for healing the trauma of people whose stories have been erased, distorted, or ignored.

~~~

In the corporate world, Lush cosmetics is a great example of a company that has stepped forward toward an opportunity for healing. While they have always been known for products that are ethically sourced and low-waste, they are increasingly taking steps to address racial justice. In 2020, they decided to shine a spotlight on how communities of color were disproportionately impacted by COVID-19, and they invited me to speak about how the pandemic was impacting Native American communities and to amplify the COVID-19 response fund that I had launched. For Indigenous People's Day, they allowed me to take over their Instagram account, with its 4.2 million followers, for half a day; their tagline is "creating a cosmetic revolution to save the planet." This gave me the opportunity to highlight various Indigenous activists and campaigns across the United States as well as to celebrate our culture with spoken word, song, and dance. Meanwhile, they invited me to offer Decolonizing Wealth workshops to their management.

As I see it, Lush is modeling three kinds of medicine. First, their corporate philanthropy is prioritizing Indigenous folks and people of color. Second, they're using their platform to amplify marginalized voices. And third, they're working to model their values internally. Who doesn't love a company that is showing up in this way *and* makes a fantastic bath bomb?

In fact, in 2020, corporations surprised many of us by taking the lead in the response to systemic racism, doing even more than the philanthropic world. Businesses contributed more than half of the $5.9 billion pledged by institutional grantmakers and other large donors. For example, PepsiCo pledged to create a $25 million scholarship program for Black students. According to the *Chronicle of Philanthropy*, "That [$5.9 billion] figure . . . surpasses the total committed to racial justice over the past nine years combined."[1]

~~~

Another example that I came across was museums and libraries. These are the places that are the repositories of our inventions, our history, and our art—either exhibited as artifacts or described in the pages of books. There are several layers to the wealth in these institutions.

The most obvious kinds of wealth are ancient, priceless pieces or precious objects made of gold and jewels, for example, that are displayed behind reinforced glass and protected by high-tech security systems and guards. A lot of those artifacts were stolen from their cultures of origin by the original colonizers. There are approximately 90,000 pieces from Africa in French museums and cultural institutions.[2] The British Museum has 8 million items in its collection, including sacred objects from all over the world, and more than 6,000 human remains. "Not everything was acquired illegally," notes an article about the British Museum in *The Economist*. "Some items were bought, exchanged or received as gifts—though there's a question as to how freely a gift is given, if it's handed over to a man at the head of a platoon of bayonets."[3]

As Masum Momoya, a former curator for the Smithsonian Institution who now works in philanthropy funding the arts, commented:

> Most of the cultural institutions that we have today were born out of either projects of colonialism, projects of nationalism and nation building, or education in a very narrow sense. This moment is calling on them to do some internal work to decolonize themselves as institutions, to confront their own racism and systemic oppression, and to grapple with things like repatriation of artifacts and things that were taken as part of the projects of colonization, missionization, exploration.
>
> I think not responding to those things will have dire consequences for the future of cultural institutions. No longer can these kinds of questions

about slavery, empire, colonization, extraction of land, exploitation of people—which museums have been a part of throughout history—no longer can those questions be swept under the rug.[4]

Then there is the question of whose art is displayed as significant (white European male painters much?) or how history is depicted, which is a kind of informational power that's really important when these institutions are used to educate people, especially young people. What kind of impact does it make to see no paintings by women of color when you're a little brown girl visiting the National Gallery? What message is sent when Africans are depicted as primitive and savage by a history museum? What is it like for an Indigenous child to be taught the names of Christopher Columbus's ships in school but not the traditional names of the land they are on? What does it indicate when most of the library books, especially the ones included in school curricula, are all written by the same kind of person?

Then there is the layer of access: Who gets to come inside and absorb the contents? Who is made to feel welcome? Many museums don't actually feel like places that welcome everyone. Even if reduced ticket prices are available—which is not always the case or communicated freely—the spaces themselves often feel like they're made with elite visitors in mind. They're a good example of what I describe as ivory towers.

Whose medicine might be found in museums and libraries? One example is the story of Congolese activist Emery Mwazulu Diyabanza. He is on a mission to bring objects from French museums back to their rightful homes in Africa. His approach: just walk up to the artifact in question, take hold of it, and walk away with it. He's done so a number of times in museums in France and in Holland, always livestreaming video of himself as he does so, as a way to call attention to the issue of restitution. When security personnel intercept him, he declares, "I don't need to ask a thief permission to retrieve a stolen object." Each time, the object has been reclaimed by the museum and Diyabanza has been arrested, sometimes resulting in a fine. At the time of this writing, he is awaiting trial for three instances of "attempted theft," but he vows to continue his symbolic actions.

"People have to understand that if someone stole their heritage, they would react as I am now," Diyabanza says. "Many of my ancestors died protecting these items: they were beheaded. They refused to accept that these objects be taken, and they were killed. Their pain is inside me."[5]

There is no question that there is momentum building around the push to make the former colonizers return stuff. As reported in *The Economist*:

> In 2017 France's president, Emmanuel Macron, declared the return of African heritage to Africa a "top priority" (though by the end of 2019 only one object had been returned). A report published the following year, commissioned by him, recommended that all objects obtained during the colonial era be restored to their country of origin unless there was proof they had been acquired legitimately. Stéphane Martin, president of the Musée de Quai Branly, an anthropological museum in Paris, decried the report in an interview with Le Monde as an act of "self-flagellation." But the French inquiry stirred the waters. The British Museum has since received multiple requests, from Ethiopia, Nigeria and Chile among others, to hand back disputed items.[6]

The restitution of the dead is especially important, given how many cultures honor their ancestors and the place in which they are buried or kept.

But you don't have to engage in action as flamboyant as Diyabanza in order to do decolonizing work. If you are one of the people who fund these cultural institutions, or the people who direct them and curate them, you have a lot of power.

As an example of a museum using its power to preserve white privilege and protect white fragility, Masum shared the story of the Museum of Contemporary Art Cleveland, which in the spring of 2020 canceled a planned exhibition by the artist Shaun Leonardo, known for his drawings of police brutality against Black and brown boys and men. The museum canceled the show without even consulting the artist, saying by way of explanation that they weren't sure that they would be able to handle the backlash, the controversy, the community reactions.[7] Essentially, the museum censored him. Talk about amplifying harm! Those curators and directors had an opportunity to do healing with that exhibit, and they blew it.

Other people who work in these institutions, like librarians, museum staff, and guards, also might find their medicine here. Even all of us who patronize these institutions might. We can leave feedback and tell them what we want them to do—after all, many of them are public institutions, and we're the public. All of us can have a hand in making sure that the wealth of these institutions is used for healing rather than to harm.

Access is wealth. Literacy is wealth. Information is wealth, too. All can be used as medicine. For instance, libraries are the primary access to information, and even to the internet, for a lot of low-income people. Libraries function as community centers, safe spaces and counseling offices, and even employment agencies—many people rely on librarians to help them navigate job listings or fill out complicated forms and applications for government benefits such as disability pay or unemployment support. Librarians sometimes even help people create and print out résumés. So librarians have a real opportunity to be healers, and this is one of the reasons why it's important that they come from the community they're serving and really understand the needs of people in the community. As it turns out, less than 20 percent of library directors are people of color.

I learned that fact when I spoke to Tracie Hall, the executive director of the American Library Association (ALA). As the first Black woman to hold that position, Tracie is determined to bring what she terms "liberation frameworks" to "the information industrial complex."

"There are over sixteen thousand public libraries across the United States, if we include branches; more libraries than we have McDonald's," she told me. "The decision-makers who are going to drive the next era of librarianship have a responsibility to get in step with our communities and our constituents. The ALA, like other elite Western institutions, has to grapple with formidable barriers to racial and ethnic diversity, including the expectation that the primary decision-makers have a master's degree."

That sure sounds a lot like an ivory tower institution. Tracie has been working on dismantling the colonizer mindset in her field. In June of 2020, the ALA and several other library associations, including the American Association of Law Libraries, the Medical Library Association, and the Society of American Archivists, took responsibility for past racism and formally pledged their commitment to equity, diversity, and inclusion.

~~~~

A final form of medicine I'll highlight here is land. One simple act of decolonization and healing that I am seeing happen with increasing frequency is simply to acknowledge the original name of the land on which you are living, working, or standing, and to acknowledge its original inhabitants. This might mean you need to start with the act of finding out who were the original owners of the land to which you have access. Which Indigenous people historically made their homes there, and are any of them still around? Every event I do begins with an acknowledgment of the land and the people who originally made it their home.

Another way to repair the harms associated with stolen land is to get involved in projects that put pressure on the governments of cities and counties to take their vacant lands and transfer them into the hands of communities via vehicles like community land trusts, which are democratic, multistakeholder organizations that own the land for the permanent benefit of the community.

But if you're *really* committed to healing, and you own land, you can give it back. There are those who say that using the term "decolonization" for anything less than the full "repatriation of Indigenous land and life" is counter-productive.[8] As extreme as this may sound, after the first edition of *Decolonizing Wealth* came out, this exact scenario happened. People began contacting me and asking me to take gifts not just of money but of land and properties worth millions and millions of dollars and to get them into Native hands. I didn't even know how to accept and redistribute these kinds of gifts, but I've had to learn.

The time for reparations is now, and there are a number of Black and Indigenous land sovereignty efforts happening. One campaign, called LANDBACK, sprang up in August 2020. It was catalyzed by the powerful moment when Native land defenders blocked the road to Mount Rushmore to prevent the July Fourth event that Donald Trump had planned to hold on sacred land in the Black Hills. Nearly two dozen land defenders were arrested, including Nick Tilsen, the head of the all-Indigenous organization NDN Collective. In addition to blocking Trump's event, NDN called for the closure of Mount Rushmore—"an international symbol of white supremacy"—and the return of all public lands to the original stewards. That final demand—the return of all public lands—is the core of the LANDBACK movement.

Krystal Two Bulls, LANDBACK's campaign director, says:

> As systems of colonization, oppression and white supremacy start to become dismantled, getting Indigenous lands back into Indigenous hands is necessary. Truth is, that all systems and institutions of oppression that uphold white supremacy were built on top of stolen land by stolen people; so to truly achieve racial justice and move into a revolutionary moment, we have to talk about how racial injustice on this continent began with settler colonialism, the theft of Indigenous lands, and the genocide of Indigenous people.[9]

The LANDBACK movement isn't an eviction notice for settlers; it's an invitation to use this form of wealth to heal the long legacy of exploitation and a lack of safety.

If you are interested in returning land you own to Indigenous people, the next step is to begin building relationships with local tribes and see if there is interest. One option is to donate the land to a nonprofit while still retaining the ability to live on the land during your or your family members' lifetime(s) and to donate what is called a "remainder interest" in the land while retaining what is called a "life estate." Another way to move toward land repatriation is to sell acres of land and give the proceeds to support ongoing Indigenous-led organizing or land return projects. Philanthropic funding can also be directed to buy up land and hand over control of it to communities to collectively own and steward it for future generations.

The more I hear stories like these, the more my eyes are opened to how many kinds of resources or wealth or access can be transformed into healing. The medicine that called most loudly and forcefully to me was money, but your medicine—your invitation to step into the work of decolonization—could be almost anything. All it takes is for you to recognize the opportunity: that something in your workplace or life can be leveraged as medicine, for healing. The "Discussion Guide and Resources" section at the end of the book (new to this second edition) might spark something for you.

Your own invitation to use something as medicine might not seem like it's as significant as taking on an institution or sector that's giving away billions of dollars. It might just be a one-on-one conversation; it might just be planting the first seeds, which don't immediately lead to a dramatic shift. That's OK. Just trust that, in some way, it will make a difference. Anyone who is willing to step forward and call out the colonizer dynamics of separation and exploitation, to speak truth to power, can be part of the healing process. What's your medicine?

CHAPTER EIGHT

Story as Medicine

There's one kind of medicine that everyone has access to, and that's your own story. Sharing your story—especially if you come from a people who have been marginalized or even made invisible by mainstream culture—can be an incredibly powerful form of healing. Often, the only thing that can comfort someone who has experienced trauma is the story of someone else who went through something similar and made it through. Stories help us make sense of our lives and of the world.

It's just as important to share your own story as it is to hear the stories of others. It's not uncommon that after hearing the way others tell their story and telling your own story repeatedly, you change how you tell your story. You may, for example, shift from thinking of yourself as a pitiful victim to instead considering yourself a resilient survivor. When you understand the story of which you're part and the roles you are capable of playing, you can heal wounds within yourself and others. As some Native elders say, "Those who know the stories are the healers."

There's a beautiful project called the Human Library, which started in Denmark and is now active in 80 countries around the world. Rather than lend books, this "library" lends people. Each person who volunteers to be a "book" represents a stigmatized group and agrees to share their story and answer questions to help challenge stereotypes and biases. You can borrow a refugee. You can borrow a homeless person. You can borrow someone with attention deficit/hyperactivity disorder. You can borrow an obese person, a bisexual person, an autistic person, a transperson. Human rights advocate Ronni Abergel, one of the Human Library's founders, says the healing goes both ways:

> All of our books are volunteers, some have been with us for many years, and hearing about how they constantly learn things about themselves when readers ask them something they have not been asked before just gives us joy. They are getting to know themselves, as well as processing their traumas and experiences, through these dialogues. It is a beautiful process to witness, and it is also a sign that the conversations between reader and book are genuine.[1]

The motto of the Human Library is "Unjudge someone," and currently they're working toward a global event called Unjudgment Day. I love it.

For Native Americans, our modern-day genocide is invisibility. By sharing our stories, we remind people that we're still here. It's a way of bringing visibility to Native issues, and it can disrupt stereotypes and inaccurate ideas that people have about Native Americans.

You might be telling yourself that your story is too ordinary, but I can't emphasize enough how meaningful it is to come out and stand in the light so others can see you, take heart, and take courage. Those were the words of my "auntie" Tia Oros Peters, who runs the Seventh Generation Fund and has committed her life to supporting Indigenous people, especially women. She opened my book launch party with a blessing and a prayer: "We are coming out and standing in the light around the change that needs to be made." Her words were so powerful, they still give me chills.

I never could have imagined how many people my story would touch. When I got into philanthropy, it felt like I gained access to significant power to heal people, yet that hardly holds a candle to the power that came with sharing my story.

It all started at the book launch party on October 15, 2018, in New York. I wanted it to be not just a celebration of the book but also a way to elevate my community. Everything came together beautifully, like it was ordained. We secured the Highline Ballroom in the Meatpacking District, and then we booked Anthony Ramos and Jasmine Cephas Jones, who were both in the original cast of *Hamilton* and have since become Hollywood stars. I reached out to Jeremy Salazar, a Navajo artist based in Albuquerque whom I'd been following on Instagram, who paints portraits of Native warriors. He'd never been to New York City and we'd never met in person, but he agreed to ship a bunch of his paintings on ahead so we could fill the entire upstairs of the ballroom with his work. "You better believe there will be price tags on them," I told him. "It's New York freaking City. Charge people. Sell your art." The comedian and activist Baratunde Thurston agreed to be our emcee. I reached out to Tony Duncan, who is a San Carlos Apache and Hidatsa world champion hoop dancer and toured with Nelly Furtado. The night of the launch, dressed in traditional Indian regalia, he performed to techno music. Mind-blowing.

Tickets sold out, and when the doors opened that night, there was a line down the block to get in. I had recruited young people from the Center for Native American Youth to be our social media ambassadors and to sell the #decolonizer T-shirts that premiered that night and went huge. Right there in the middle of noisy New York City, we created a spiritual grounding that was undeniably Indigenous, and everyone could feel it. A lot of people said they'd never experienced anything like it. It felt way bigger than just about me and the book. Coming out of that event, something had been birthed. It set us on fire.

From that magical launch through the end of 2020, I spoke to more than 60,000 people, in all kinds of spaces, from foundation boardrooms to conference keynotes, from university auditoriums to gatherings of investors and entrepreneurs, to corporate headquarters where an entire staff had gathered. Everywhere I went, people said how much the book meant to them—thousands and thousands of people. People talked about finding healing, and hope, and inspiration. They told me it's a message for this moment in time—that *Decolonizing Wealth* gave words to feelings that they hadn't been able to express before now. I had never expected that my story would resonate so far and wide.

One of the most memorable invites of all was probably to the Skoll World Forum on Social Entrepreneurship, which took place in Oxford, England, in April 2019. On the way there, I made a quick stop in London, where I met with a local group of funders and nonprofit leaders and learned that their conversation about colonial crimes and racial healing is somewhat behind our own in the United States. It felt like our meeting ignited something they were longing for, deeply. They were so grateful to have the chance to talk openly about colonization, racial discrimination, and trauma. It was powerful to feel like I was contributing to the liberation of people, and I knew in that moment that this movement to decolonize wealth had become global.

Then I arrived in the famous university town of Oxford, with its picture-perfect Gothic spires and old stone college buildings. When I walked on the stage to deliver my speech during the opening plenary, I had to pinch myself, being there in that grand old theater with its multiple balconies, like a gilded wedding cake. I was standing in the very same spot where Bono had recently spoken, addressing people representing dozens of countries. But I wasn't even nervous. I had the same feeling as back when I'd been in seminary and delivered sermons, that sense of being a vessel for something to move through me. I could feel the energy of love and power flow through me, and then the reciprocity as it transformed the audience and came back toward me.

That magical feeling has been with me as I told my story everywhere, whether it was a smaller group of 15 or a stage with 15,000 people in the audience. To be clear, it hasn't always been comfortable for me in those elite spaces. There was the president of a large foundation who introduced me by saying that the only thing she knew about Native Americans was that she'd played cowboys and Indians as a child, and the Indians always died. *What?* Or I've been in conversations with institutions that I know are actively harming Indigenous communities. In moments like these, I have had to bite my tongue and take deep breaths, so that I could be strategic about my influence in those circles.

In my home state of North Carolina, there was an event at the Bank of America headquarters, organized by Valaida Fullwood, a wonderful woman who is a longtime colleague and friend, a champion of Black giving circles. Before the event, I received an email from someone who said he would not be attending because he would never step foot in the Bank of America building, given how much harm the bank had caused his community. I respected his choice, but it was clear to me that with the work I am called to do, I must be willing to go anywhere with this message. I will go into the belly of the beast, because where better to disrupt the status quo? I don't feel that I have the luxury of saying no. If they will have me, if they want to hear my story, I will go there and tell it.

At a Decolonizing Wealth event in Hollywood, I partnered with Crystal Echo Hawk to secure Native art for the venue and to get the invites to the right folks. Crystal founded an organization called IllumiNative, which works to change perceptions and to bring visibility to Native Americans, especially through narratives in media. At one point during the event, she walked up to me and grabbed me and said, "Oh my God, Edgar. This event—*this* is narrative change. This is narrative change." That was exactly what I was going for. To showcase the work of Native American artists, musicians, and cultural influencers on a rooftop filled with powerful folks who are controlling the story and the money in the entertainment industry, to bring the message of decolonizing, truth, healing, reconciliation, and racial justice front and center. We were bringing our community into a space where we have been extremely invisible, into a space where stories and stereotypes have actually harmed us, and shifting that by showing something different. We showed them that Natives are contemporary—we are very much alive and well and are leading across all aspects of modern society. The future is Indigenous, and we must be in control of our own stories, moving forward.

Hollywood and the broader terrain of media at large offer so many opportunities for using story as medicine. Until recently, those who were working for dignity, justice, and equity hadn't really engaged with popular culture. But the stories told in popular culture have serious consequences.

They justify the status quo, they establish norms around all kinds of issues, from race relations to immigration, from the ideal of what success looks like to the ideal of what safety looks like—think of how many police-glorifying crime shows have there been! These stories impact whom we think of as "us" and "them," as "welfare queens" or "thugs," as deserving or undeserving. They justify institutions and policies and solutions and keep us from imagining other paths by making those seem inevitable. Talk about power!

One group that's been doing amazing work to leverage that power is the Pop Culture Collaborative, a $25 million fund created to help artists, activists, and organizations leverage the power of pop culture to drive authentic narratives on people of color, immigrants, refugees, and Muslims. Through partnerships between the social justice sector, on the one hand, and the entertainment, advertising, and media industries, on the other, the collaborative helps transform the narrative landscape in America. It helps mainstream audiences understand the past, make sense of the present, and imagine the future of American society. Its founder and director, Bridgit Antoinette Evans, says in a Reddit comment, "Most people underestimate the role that pop culture stories like the TV shows, films, music, books, and magazines we love influence how we make decisions and relate to each other in the world. But the power is real."[2]

Indeed, beyond their impact in shifting perceptions, shattering stereotypes, and creating empathy on the individual level, the stories of our lives actually carry the seeds of potential for changing complicated systems like white supremacy and patriarchy. The key is to connect our personal stories with larger narratives. Veteran organizer Marshall Ganz trains people who work on community issues to develop their "public story," because once you step out into the public eye, if don't tell your story, someone else will.

A good public story, according to Ganz, "is drawn from the series of choice points that have structured the 'plot' of your life—the challenges you faced, choices you made, and outcomes you experienced."[3] Why did it feel like a challenge? Why did you make the choice you did? Where did you get the courage to make the choice? How did the outcome impact you? What can it teach us?

From there, you connect your personal story to what Ganz calls the "story of us" and "the story of now." The story of us is the story of the community with which you're identifying: How do your personal challenges and choices reflect the broader situation and legacy of that community? The story of now is the narrative of the larger challenges and choices going on in the world at this time, whether that's authoritarian, antidemocratic, and overtly white supremacist movements, the consequences of the pandemic, or the threats from climate chaos. This is how a personal story links to a movement: identifying the big challenges we face and calling for specific choices and actions that will move the dial.

In this moment, when people in our country (and in the wider world) are so extremely divided along lines of political allegiance as well as of race and economics and gender, we desperately need medicine that will bring us back together as one human race, to make us feel we are all related. I truly believe that story is a powerful form of medicine to heal those divides—and it's a medicine that *everyone* can access.

PART THREE

How to Heal

In order to embrace a new paradigm of *connect, relate, belong,* instead of *divide, control, exploit,* we first have to heal. The metaphor of healing reflects my stance in the reform versus revolution debate. Some will say that the colonial system of wealth consolidation based on white supremacy has caused so much damage and suffering and is so intrinsically rotten that anything related to it, including the ostensibly altruistic worlds of philanthropy or aid, cannot be fixed, cannot be trusted, should not be saved. Those voices would burn the system to the ground and start fresh. I empathize with that perspective, yet I believe there are parts of the system worth holding on to. The both/and stance is how Native Americans have survived colonization. Evolution occurs both by holding on to the adaptations that keep us thriving and by abandoning the elements that keep us *from* thriving.

~~~

Every time we contemplate huge goals like social justice and equity, or a slightly smaller goal like real evolution inside the field of finance or philanthropy, we encounter beliefs about what is possible. What is pragmatic and realistic and what is idealistic or utopian? I expect that some of the Seven Steps to Healing will be considered radical by large, long-standing institutions. There will be those who say my proposals are too far out there, a fantasy, pie in the sky.

This is the tension that we face in evolving. People who rely on the current system are afraid to dismantle it, because when we're out in the middle of the ocean during the perfect storm, no land in sight, who's going to poke holes in the only lifeboat we have, even if it's a terrible vessel?

There is always this abyss. On one side of it are the pragmatists, saying, *This is just the way things are; we have to make the best of it; things never change; it's human nature.* On the other side of the abyss are the idealists, imagining another world, building utopias. Some of the hardest work involves crisscrossing the abyss, understanding both positions, and seeking ways to bridge them. Evolving a complex set of systems, like white supremacy and capitalism, and long-standing institutions like governments, banks, and foundations, requires bridge builders who can envision opportunities for change and lead with compassion.

Marginalization and oppression seem to stifle the imagination—among both those who suffer and those who benefit from the current transactional systems of wealth. Unfortunately, the majority of our groundbreaking and inspiring idealists are part of the powerful elite, holding all the high cards of privilege; think of players like Elon Musk and Richard Branson. We need to populate the idealist side of the abyss with different kinds of people, who have different visions of future possibilities. Much has been written about how colonizers rewrite the history of the places and the people they colonize. Part of keeping total control is staking a claim on the past. But colonizers also control the future. They control what is imaginable.

The idealists yell over the abyss that the sheep stuck in the status quo are cowards. The pragmatists shout back that the idealists are out of touch with reality. One response to the pragmatists is to question their certainty that this is indeed reality. We can be like Neo in *The Matrix*, taking the red pill and seeing the constructed world as an illusion. "The willingness to own up to the fictional nature of our story is where the healing begins," writes Peter Block in his book on civic engagement, *Community*.[1]

White supremacy is just a story humans created. Race is just a story humans created. Resources as scarce, greed as an inescapable aspect of human nature, and money as the root of evil—all these are stories. Over time, these stories have become so solidified and familiar and "true" that they began limiting our view of the world and our choices. They became beliefs, articles of faith. Yet our beliefs are just one perspective, and the more rigid our perspective, the more alternative perspectives we miss.

Once we understand that the stories are optional—choices we made—we can choose to let go of any beliefs that limit us. Every obstacle can be incorporated and can become an ally, another beautiful aspect of authentic wholeness. A free imagination is key to overcoming limiting beliefs.

The central question at the foundation of much science fiction—What if . . . ?—is a legitimate tool of healing and reconstructing the world. Even just asking the question opens us to radically different possible realities and can lead to healing, to a greater sense of dignity and purpose.

The film *Black Panther* allowed us to imagine a fictionalized nation of unfathomable wealth that refuses to play by the rules of *divide, control, exploit,* to imagine a world where Black people triumph. #WakandaForever.

What if funders could help restore a perfect world? What if money could be medicine instead of what divides us? What if rather than using wealth to cause further harm, we followed the Seven Steps to Healing?

Grieve

It's not what you were expecting from a book about wealth. Yet before we can move forward with using money as medicine, to heal divides and restore balance, we have to grieve. Grieving requires softening your self-protective defense mechanisms enough to feel, getting beyond the denial, numbness, righteousness, apathy, and other obstacles we have put in place to avoid the depths of pain. The humanity that was previously made invisible must be made visible again.

We who were colonized have to grieve for the people, the cultures, and the lands that were forcibly taken from us. We have to mourn the suffering of our ancestors who were cheated, humiliated, raped, and killed. We have to grieve for hundreds of years of our being disrespected, displaced, and dispossessed. We have to grieve for our children, who embody the trauma of this history, and now have the decks stacked against them as they face the future.

Those who have embodied and sustained the colonizer virus also have much to grieve for. The fear, anxiety, and mistrust that characterizes being a member of the 1 percent is no joke. The survival mechanisms they often adopt include staying walled off, physically and emotionally disconnected, and well medicated.

White people have to grieve the guilt that accompanies whiteness. You cannot and must not opt out of whiteness. You have to grapple with the messiness of the privilege. You have to come and collect your people.

Settlers and their descendants have to grieve the lives of their ancestors, the culture that made their acts of domination and exploitation even imaginable, possible, and acceptable. What confused, numbed, dissociated hell it must have been for them, on a deep level, even if they enjoyed benefits on other levels. Hurting people hurt others (something else I learned growing up watching Oprah). Generations down the line must grieve the culture of the present, which perpetuates the colonizer mindset of domination and exploitation.

Trust me, I know that there are those who are not ready to consider the suffering of colonizers and oppressors, let alone forgive them or welcome them. However, the Native principle of All My Relations means that settlers are our relatives too. It means our interdependence is inescapable, so we may as well acknowledge each other's trauma and engage in healing together.

Stephen Jenkinson, a white Canadian trained in theology at Harvard, best known for his writing and speaking about his work with people who are dying, has also reflected profoundly on what it is to be a non-Indigenous, a settler. He calls it being an "orphan," a term that includes all the people uprooted from their ancestral homes for whatever reasons, whether it was by choice or not. The European settlers who came to the Americas are orphans, but so are the slaves they brought over, and so are the people lured to America's shores in recent decades by the promise of work, wealth, and the American Dream. They are all orphans, in his worldview.

"Orphans are not people who have no parents. They are people who don't know their parents, who cannot go to them from here. Ours is a culture built upon the ruthless foundation of mass migration, but it is more so now a culture of people unable to say who their people are. In that way we are, relentlessly, orphans."[1]

Orphans broke the ties to their lands of origin, to the bones of their ancestors, to their old ways. The grief that this has caused is enormous, yet it is almost never acknowledged. In the wake of the choice to abandon, to sever, to forget, Jenkinson believes, is the shame of secretly believing you come from nothing that has merit. First and foremost, Jenkinson calls for sorrow and grieving among orphans, acknowledging the profound longing for connection and purpose and ancestry.

Reframing colonizer-settlers as orphans and cultivating empathy for them will probably rub some people the wrong way. I get it. It's not just about turning the other cheek, taking the higher road, or being more virtuous, though. It's literally a pragmatic choice in order to end the cycles: the cycles of pain and hurt; the cycles of *divide, control,* [and above all,] *exploit.* According to those who work to heal abusers, the point of recognizing the victimization of perpetrators is not to excuse, forgive, or in any way diminish the destructiveness of their actions but rather to develop an accurate understanding of how oppression works, how it is sustained and recreated over generations, how to end it.

So all of us have to grieve how the culture of domination and exploitation took us over, no matter the color of our skin or how we came to live in this country. We have to grieve all that we've done since being infected with the colonizer virus—how exploitation was at the foundation of how we earned and used and managed money, how transactions replaced relationships, how we lost sight of our common humanity.

In her book *Medicine Stories*, *curandera* and historian Aurora Levins Morales writes:

> Ours is a society that does not do grieve well or easily, and what is required to face trauma is the ability to mourn, fully and deeply, all that has been taken from us. But mourning is painful and we resist giving way to it, distract ourselves with put-on toughness out of pride. . . . What is so dreadful is that to transform the traumatic we must re-enter it fully, and allow the full weight of grief to pass through our hearts. It is not possible to digest atrocity without tasting it first, without assessing on our tongues the full bitterness of it.[2]

~~~

One of my conversations while writing this book was with Hilary Giovale, a trustee of the Geo Family Foundation. A white woman who became involved in philanthropy after marrying into wealth, she's become something of an advocate for awakening other white folks to white privilege and believes that white people absolutely need to be saved from white supremacy. Hilary told me:

> About a year and a half ago, I developed an interest in learning about my ancestry, because the story for most of us white folks starts here in America, with no recollection of what happened before our

arrival. My understanding had been that my people had come from Scotland and Ireland several generations ago, and that we were very poor people, seeking a new beginning. Although this is true of my most recent ancestors, I now understand that focusing on this story while excluding the big picture is part of the mythology that helps justify white supremacy.

I came to realize that I had an ancestor who arrived in 1739 from Scotland, and he landed in North Carolina. His grandson received a land grant. I was horrified, as it became clear to me that it was land stolen from Indigenous people of North Carolina. Later, that grandson went down to Mississippi and Louisiana, and he and some of his descendants owned slaves. There were records of slaves' names and how much they were worth in a book of family genealogy. Again, it was devastating. I had to go through a process of deep grieving. . . .

When we white people start to learn about this history and to build relationships with people who are still living the intergenerational historical trauma of colonization on a daily basis, a lot of us are totally paralyzed by guilt and by shame, and we don't know what to do, so we have to check out. We have to put our blinders on and become numb to all of that. I see that whole dynamic as part of the reason that we're still so separate today. . . .

The first thing you have to do is understand that you have white privilege. When you understand that you have it, you are going to feel bad. You're going to feel some discomfort, guilt, and shame. This is part of the process and cannot be short-circuited. Engaging these uncomfortable feelings opens space for different ways of interacting with diverse people and projects. It creates possibilities for healing to happen on all sides.[3]

Philanthropist Peter Buffett talked to me about how it was no coincidence that the first philanthropic organizations were created in the Gilded Age, against the backdrop of industrialization, which, alongside creating enormous concentrations of wealth, also led to anxiety, depression, and existential crises. For most people, work had gone from mostly autonomous productive activities that involved a sense of purpose and satisfaction, like craftsmanship or farming, to being a cog in the assembly line of industry somewhere, lacking any sense of agency or power. "It led to one hundred fifty years of purposelessness, especially for men. The most powerful tried to put a salve on these losses with philanthropy, but the losses were huge. When you unpack this, there's a lot of pain."[4]

~~~~

Organizations, companies, and institutions can support the grieving process. Once upon a time, this idea would have been laughed at as unprofessional or indulgent, but there is increasing evidence that intentionally creating and holding space for grief can make an organization more productive. Organizational designers now recommend that pain be publicly acknowledged and mourned. Sharing the grief destigmatizes the feelings, validates them, and allows for healing.

The day after the election of Donald Trump in 2016, I was on a flight to Atlanta to attend Facing Race, a national conference of racial justice organizers and advocates. Days before, I had been confident that I was going to be attending a victorious celebration with a thousand of my closest friends in philanthropy and the movement. Instead, we boarded the flight like a funeral procession. We sat soberly, in extreme grief. As we gathered in Atlanta, no one could fathom the country's choice of hateful, backwards-thinking leadership. A roomful of visionaries was unable to see through the tears. We spent those few days together talking through the election results, crying, and beginning to process.

It was a lifesaver for me. I can think of no better place to have been in such a time. In the weeks following, I heard stories about how some foundations held space for grieving, while others did not even acknowledge the immense sorrow being carried by staff. In many cases, staff self-organized to hold each other up. Spaces for grief validate us and help to start the process of healing.

Indeed, by 2020, the suffering and devastation that was augmented by the Trump administration reached an all-time high. The year 2020 was the first time I've experienced grieving at a collective scale. As a CNN headline in May summarized it: "Two Deadly Viruses Are Killing Americans: COVID-19 and Racism."

There were so many losses, and so many people were deprived of the opportunity to comfort one another in person, or to have the closure that comes with attending a funeral. As with so much else that was laid bare and revealed during this terrible year, our need for developing more support in coping with grief became apparent, and although it's a tragic way to realize this fact, the realization gives me some hope that as a culture we might seize the opportunity to grieve more openly and more productively.

An organizational design consultant in post-apartheid South Africa commented on how much of the emphasis in institutions is on articulating an exciting vision of the future.

> [But] selling the vision of a new, exciting future to people who are still in grief is akin to telling a grieving husband at the grave of his wife to marvel at the beauty and virtues of potential wives standing around the grave. Such thinking ignores the loss, hurt, and pain that comes with change. The widower must first grieve his spouse before he can see and appreciate new possibilities.[5]

Susan David, a psychologist at Harvard Medical School and author of *Emotional Agility*, argues that workplaces focus on positivity to the detriment of well-being and that the suppression of negative emotions can be harmful. "Teams that feel safe enough to articulate discontent or talk about frustration are the most high-functioning teams," she notes. "When we only allow some emotions, we create a huge amount of emotional labor. We also create a situation for individuals that is psychologically unhealthy and undermines the organization's ability to learn and function more effectively."[6] It only makes sense that if people are busy suppressing some parts of their thoughts and emotions, they won't be able to participate or focus fully.

Philanthropy has a culture of politeness. On the surface, everyone gets along and seems happy to work together, but often there are simmering issues that cannot be addressed because it is taboo to "rock the boat." Pushing back is frowned upon. Being nice isn't a problem per se, but when people cannot speak their minds or address what concerns them, we may miss out on the best thinking, and feelings of bitterness can begin to fester.

The role for leaders is to create a safe space for vulnerability by sharing their own trauma and grief and by modeling listening, compassion, and empathy. These developments are part of the shift toward enabling people to bring their full selves to work. Grieving needs to happen both on an individual level and within all the institutions along the loans-to-gifts spectrum.

STEP TWO

Apologize

Apologizing turns us from the inward focus of grief, outward to the Others who were harmed. Around money, apologies are due for where the wealth came from—almost always from the theft of land and resources, the exploitation of slaves and low-wage workers. Apologies are due for how that wealth was maneuvered out of appropriate taxation—off shore, into havens, into foundations—and shirked its responsibility in paying for roads, bridges, public schools, firefighters, eldercare, and so on. Apologies are due for the majority of investments, which support harmful industries, practices, and regimes. Apologies are due for the greed and pettiness that characterize a lot of our everyday behavior and interactions around money, all of which arise out of the separation paradigm, the myth of scarcity, this idea that we're not together in this thing called life.

Apologizing requires that white people of wealth snap out of their paralyzing white fragility and guilt and just step up. It requires that people of color and Indigenous people dismantle their internalized oppression and admit that they, too, were infected by the colonizer virus. Basically, it requires everyone to grow up and take responsibility for their actions, in order to move forward.

Pumla Gobodo-Madikizela is a South African psychologist and academic who participated in the South African Truth and Reconciliation Commission. The TRC was a restorative justice process between victims and perpetrators of apartheid-era violence in South Africa. In her book *A Human Being Died That Night*, she beautifully describes the experiences of a society coming to terms with its past:

> A genuine apology focuses on the feelings of the other rather than on how the one who is apologizing is going to benefit in the end. It seeks to acknowledge full responsibility for an act, and does not use self-serving language to justify the behavior of the person asking forgiveness. A sincere apology does not seek to erase what was done. No amount of words can undo past wrongs. Nothing can ever reverse injustices committed against others. But an apology pronounced in the context of horrible acts has the potential for transformation. It clears or "settles" the air in order to begin reconstructing the broken connections between two human beings.[1]

Decent people and decent societies admit when they've done wrong. There are places in the world that have made a good-faith effort to acknowledge their mistakes and at least begin the process of apologizing; post-apartheid South Africa and Germany after World War II come to mind.

In 2008, in front of Parliament, the prime minister of Australia, Kevin Rudd, issued a formal apology to Aborigines for federal policies that "inflicted profound grief, suffering, and loss on these our fellow Australians."[2] Canada is another place, like South Africa, where a truth and reconciliation process has taken place, in Canada's case around the experiences of Native peoples. The Truth and Reconciliation Commission of Canada was launched in 2008, following the 1996 closing of the last of their Indian boarding schools, which had removed some 150,000 Native children from their families. In the worst cases, students died. Many others experienced psychological, physical, and sexual abuse.[3]

In the United States, an official congressional apology for slavery was not made until June 2009, during President Obama's first term. In December of the same year, with little fanfare, Obama signed off on the historic Native American Apology Resolution as part of a defense appropriations spending bill, apologizing "on behalf of the people of the United States to all Native peoples for the many instances of violence, maltreatment, and neglect inflicted on Native peoples by citizens of the United States." The resolution also included a disclaimer: nothing in it authorizes or supports any legal claims against the United States. (Cue the music for "Sorry Not Sorry," by Demi Lovato.)

Native critics said that the lack of publicity around the announcement lessened its impact as an official apology. "What kind of an apology is it when they don't tell the people they are apologizing to?" asked Robert J. Coulter, executive director of the Indian Law Center. "For an apology to have any meaning at all, you do have to tell the people you're apologizing to."[4] But at least it was a start.

Then there are places that stubbornly refuse to apologize. In *The Empire Pays Back*, a British documentary that first aired in 2005, the director Robert Beckford called out the British. He posed the questions: Why has Britain made no apology for African slavery? Why was there no public monument in London on the scale of Berlin's Holocaust Memorial and museum? Why was there no recognition of how the prosperity of modern Britain was made possible by wealth extracted from Africa and Africans?[5] Given Prime Minister Tony Blair's 1997 apology to the Irish for England's role in the Potato Famine, it should be a source of enormous embarrassment that the country has never apologized for its activities in any of its former colonies, in Africa most of all. Instead, there is widespread ambivalence today among British citizens about whether or not colonization was a good thing. #sorrynotsorry

~~~~

As Peter Buffett has written, "I believe that words can change the world. On a personal level, when we say, 'I hear you' or 'I'm sorry,' worlds can change."[6]

After investigating her ancestry and discovering her own family's involvement in land theft and slavery, Hilary Giovale of the Geo Family Foundation wrote a letter acknowledging these truths and sent it to 15 of her friends, including people of color, Indigenous people, and white people. "It was very, very scary, because that's not something we talk about in America. But amazingly, I was shown a great deal of compassion. It was a beautiful process."

In becoming transparent about her ancestry, Hilary says, "My heart was calling me to apologize, but for some time, I still felt ambivalent about it. I was worried that any apology I could give would seem insincere, insufficient, or that it would generate fresh pain and inflict further harm." However, through ensuing conversations, collaborative relationships, and decolonization work, she eventually found the strength to apologize. This is the apology she works with today:

To my Indigenous Relatives and Relatives of Color:
I apologize for my ignorance of the harm that came
to you and the horrors you survived through many
generations. I apologize for my unconscious racism
and white supremacy, and the pain they have
caused you. I apologize for the silent ways I gave
my own comfort priority over your existence as a
sovereign human being. When I dishonored you, I
dishonored my own humanity and the humanity
of all our children. I am sorry. I love you. Please
forgive me.

To my European-Descended Relatives: I apologize for all the times I have judged you instead of
allowing myself to feel the grief of our collective
spiritual impoverishment and cultural amnesia. I
apologize for seeing you as a monster of oppression, instead of a Child of Creation. I apologize
for disassociating from you and denying that we
are related. When I judged you, I judged my own
ancestors, my children, and myself. I am sorry. I
love you. Please forgive me.[7]

She shakes her head at the fact that it took her until
adulthood—and it took her family nine generations of
colonization—before this moment occurred in which she
finally found the courage to apologize. Yet as the civil rights
activist W. E. B. Du Bois said, "It is *never* too late to mend.
Nothing is so bad that good may not be put into it and
make it better and save it from utter loss."[8]

In September 2020, we saw one of the most comprehensive and impressive examples of a reckoning with past
failures and an apology from a business—the *Los Angeles*

Times—when the paper published a groundbreaking editorial entitled "An Examination of The Times' Failures on Race, Our Apology and a Path Forward." The editors reviewed the paper's entire history and took responsibility by, for example, admitting the paper's support of the incarceration of Japanese Americans during World War II or its contributions to anti-Mexican sentiments during the Eisenhower administration. "For at least its first 80 years, the *Los Angeles Times* was an institution deeply rooted in white supremacy and committed to promoting the interests of the city's industrialists and landowners." It ends with the unequivocal declaration: "On behalf of this institution, we apologize for *The Times*' history of racism. We owe it to our readers to do better, and we vow to do so."[9]

In 2020, then under Tracie Hall's leadership, the American Library Association released a public statement accepting and acknowledging "its role in upholding unjust systems of racism and discrimination against Black, Indigenous, and People of Color (BIPOC) within the association and the profession." Hall had read the first edition of this book, and she saw this recognition of harm and apology as a pivotal step toward building more inclusive libraries. As the oldest and largest library association in the world, the ALA is the professional association for 57,000 library executives, frontline staff, trustees, and associated stakeholders across the United States. Tracie, the first Black woman to hold the ALA's executive director position, became a librarian because of the Spectrum Scholarship Program, an initiative created in 1998 to bring more people of color to librarianship. Before coming to libraries, Tracie had worked as a program director for a homeless shelter. In her first address to the ALA's membership, Tracie dedicated her tenure to the late Black poet/activist Audre Lorde, who received her own library degree from Columbia University in 1961.

From the moment she took on her role, Tracie began asking herself how she could deploy her position and her institution as a medicine, having realized that the access to information that libraries hold is a kind of wealth in itself. She asked herself *What does reconciliation look like [for us]?* On Juneteenth—Emancipation Day for formerly enslaved people—the ALA decided to issue a formal apology. This was fitting, as Tracie noted, "because enslavement was often enforced through illiteracy." On June 19, 2020, the apology went live:

> The American Library Association (ALA) accepts and acknowledges its role in upholding unjust systems of racism and discrimination against Black, Indigenous, and People of Color (BIPOC) within the association and the profession.
>
> We recognize that the founding of our Association was not built on inclusion and equity, but instead was built on systemic racism and discrimination in many forms. We also recognize the hurt and harm done to BIPOC library workers and communities due to these racist structures.
>
> We commit to our core values, particularly equity, diversity, and inclusion, and will demonstrate this commitment by reassessing and reevaluating our role in continuing to uphold unjust, harmful systems throughout the Association and the profession. We will include ALA members, ALA staff, and the profession in our movement forward, and we are developing a plan toward becoming the inclusive association we aspire to be. . . .

We take responsibility for our past, and pledge
to build a more equitable association and library
community for future generations of library workers and supporters.[10]

What if every "ivory tower" institution followed the
example set by the libraries?

Not long ago I was at a funders meeting in Charleston,
South Carolina, where a network called Grantmakers for
Southern Progress gathered and released a new report
about funding in the South. A young white man got up to
present this report. His first slide was an image of a historic
census document from his great-grandfather, which listed
all the slaves his grandfather had owned and their names.
"I feel like people should know where I come from," the
young man said, "and I'm sorry that this is where I come
from, but I want to be a part of changing things."

There we were, in a plantation-style hotel, just blocks
from where slaves were actually sold. It had to be terri-
fying for him to stand up in front of so many Black faces
in his audience and say what he said. But it felt as if his
action brought the room together. Sure enough, later that
night I was in a car full of Black folks who had been at the
presentation. They said how moved they were, and how
they loved that young white man. Not recognizing history
is very painful for a lot of people.

I also spoke to Sara Lyons, one of the cofounders of a
Canadian nonprofit called the Circle on Philanthropy and
Aboriginal Peoples in Canada, or the Circle, for short. Its
mission is to foster more and better conversations, connections, and relationships among Aboriginal peoples and
philanthropic organizations. The Circle is urging Canada's
philanthropy community to further the work of the Truth
and Reconciliation Commission, which officially ended in

2015, and to demonstrate ongoing leadership on reconciliation and healing.

Sara told me, "The level of awareness and interest in the notion of reconciliation is really high, and foundations are really—I think genuinely—both committed to being part of change and interested in figuring out and working with others in what their piece of that is."[11] One of their initiatives has involved getting foundations to sign a Declaration of Action that commits the undersigned foundations to learn about and remember the tragedy that was the Indian residential school system experience; to "understand and acknowledge by . . . recognizing the need for an ongoing commitment to support the continuation of this multi-generational journey of healing and reconciliation"; and to "participate and act by . . . sharing our networks, our voices, and our resources to include and benefit Aboriginal peoples."[12] As Sara put it, foundations that sign it are saying "We're aware there's an unacceptable situation in terms of quality of life and political representation of Indigenous peoples, and we commit to being part of the change."

In the United States and elsewhere, the philanthropic community and the financial community, especially those in social finance, could adopt a declaration just like this, and even spearhead the creation of truth and reconciliation committees. I would love to hear funders acknowledge the reality of the situation around wealth, to say:

> This is not our money. This wealth was created on the backs of Native people, whose role was never compensated and never acknowledged. This wealth was made on the backs of enslaved Africans. This wealth was made with stolen resources on stolen land with slave labor or low-wage labor.

This wealth was stolen again when it was shielded from taxation, which would have generated revenue to pay for community improvements and programs. We acknowledge that, and we apologize. We're sorry.

Just to hear that would mean the world.

I want to be clear: just because you apologize for bad behavior does not mean you are entitled to forgiveness or reconciliation. That's a whole other part of the process. But apologizing is a necessary step before either can happen.

STEP THREE

Listen

"If you want to learn, you have to give up talking,"
Jennifer Buffett of the NoVo Foundation told me. Her
husband, Peter, added, "I've had this wonderful, privileged,
lucky life in so many ways, so I shouldn't be the one saying,
'Here's how to solve the problem.' The people who are
experiencing it should say that. What you need to do is get
really humble, and listen, and learn. . . . Transformational
change will always require challenging conversations about
'us'—not a monologue about helping 'them.'"[1]

If I had a dollar for every time someone told me that the
folks holding the purse strings don't really listen! After 16
years in the field of philanthropy, I can't believe I'm still hearing this. Every human deserves the dignity of being heard.
The lack of listening extends far beyond philanthropy and
the finance sector, of course. You could argue that the deep
political divisions in the United States are caused by and
worsened by a refusal from both sides to listen to each other
and engage in civil conversation. People need to be reminded
what it means to listen and to be able to disagree without
immediately devolving to hate and demonization. Although
funders should be devoting resources to supporting these

kinds of respectful conversations, those funders themselves must first practice better listening.

Why is it so difficult for people and institutions of wealth to listen? They believe that they know more than others and know what's best for others. They're not open to learning or being influenced. They make positive assumptions about their own abilities and negative assumptions about everyone else. This is a reflection of the power dynamic, the white savior mentality. It's about a lack of humility and a desire to be in control.

Jed Emerson, the "godfather of impact investing," says that funders are plagued by

> "mansplaining," where men, regardless of whether or not they know anything about the topic, they just go into this explanation. As a field, we suffer from that, because you've got entrepreneurs who are looking for capital, and God forbid they don't have the right answer when they're talking to a potential investor! . . .

> There's a tendency to want to always be right, to want to always have the answer, to want to always convince others of your righteousness. Those elements make for bad investing. They may make for good short-term investing, but they don't make for good long-term value creation beyond simple financial returns.[2]

Even before failing to listen, funders and investors often exert control by framing the conversation and asking only certain kinds of questions. That already places limits on what's possible, what can or cannot be said, not to mention the predominance of advice given by funders, which shuts down conversation automatically. There is rarely space for an honest dialogue about what's really going on, the challenges being faced, because everyone's putting on a happy, successful face for the one holding the purse strings. When funders ignore input from outside their walls, they stifle priceless creativity and leadership.

Organizations evolve in the direction of the questions that funders most persistently and passionately ask. Rather than asking what's wrong, what needs to be fixed, what's broken, what if philanthropy asked a community what it is most proud of and how it could support that? Questions about what is working well are energizing; their answers spread the stories of solutions and the design of those solutions.

Otto Scharmer, a professor of leadership and management at Massachusetts Institute of Technology, says that listening is key to leadership, but not just any kind of listening. He differentiates between "downloading," which is when we only hear things that confirm what we already know; "factual listening," when we filter what we hear in search of new data and evidence; "empathetic listening," which puts us in the shoes of the speaker, connecting and feeling what s/he feels; and finally, "generative listening," in which we enter almost a meditative flow state, which enables us "to connect to the highest future possibility that can emerge."[3] We need to be striving for empathetic listening 100 percent of the time in order to heal the past, and generative listening as often as we can in order to move forward and build new organizations and new culture.

Because wealth tends to have an isolating effect—which is only heightened when ivory towers are situated and built to exclude and alienate the people seeking funding—listening is key to undoing the rigid structures of colonization that keep wealth from flowing. Focused listening allows you to get a glimpse of what it is like to be someone else and to see the world through their eyes. Being able to adopt the mindset of a person with a different background than yours creates openness in you. It will challenge your assumptions and limiting beliefs. It may lead you to solutions or ideas that you would never otherwise have been able to access.

Words are important. In many traditions, there is a belief that words have a power to create reality and must be used with discretion and responsibility. Yet people communicate much more than just the *content* of what they say. People's tone of voice, their use of metaphor, their body language also tell us a lot about their experience, their identity, and their worldview. Therefore, good listening includes being:

- **open**, not predetermining the appropriate content of communications;
- **empathetic**, truly inviting in and making space for the feelings and wisdom of the speaker; and
- **holistic**, including what is said in ways that do not use words.

In fact, we could call it "listening in color," a specific way to combat the trauma of global bleaching's relentless destruction of the number of voices that were amplified and heard within the white supremacist, colonial context.

Listening in color is a superpower that you can wield to change the status quo, no matter what role you play inside an institution on the loans-to-gifts spectrum. You may have little influence over a board or CEO's funding strategy, but you can always listen with an open heart to those seeking funding. Listening attentively means holding back your own conclusions, opinions, and judgments. You do not need to jump in and say "Me too!" This just moves the focus away from the other person and back to yourself. Give them room to breathe and take risks in conversation. No monologues and no mansplaining. Replace advice with openness and curiosity.

When funders listen in color, everyone will flourish as a result.

~~~~

After the first edition of this book came out, I was invited to speak at Amazon headquarters in Seattle, during an internal conference about race they were hosting for their employees. The invitation did give me pause. Right after the book came out, Amazon had announced its plans to open a second headquarters (HQ2) in Queens, New York, which was supposed to create 25,000 jobs and to receive nearly 3 billion dollars in government subsidies in return for gracing Queens with its presence.[4] The local community had organized against it, anticipating the rising rents and gentrification that HQ2's presence would bring, and by February 2019, Amazon had backed out of it.

Ultimately, I accepted the invite, because where better to advocate for healing than from within the belly of that corporate beast, but I didn't tell any of my peers I was going there, out of fear of losing credibility. I was completely unprepared to be as impressed as I was.

Six thousand "Amazonians" attended the conference, which was happening for the second time, organized and led by people of color in leadership positions. The first thing that struck me was that I was not given any restrictions on what I could say during my presentation—they didn't tell me to stay quiet about HQ2 or all the worker's rights issues or Whole Foods employees losing health benefits when Amazon took over, or the absurd amount of money that Jeff Bezos rakes in. As it turned out, I didn't have to be the one to raise the issues, because the very first thing they did as they opened the conference was to take responsibility. "We need to be honest about how we have harmed community." They mentioned that they had made a big misstep with HQ2 and how they entered that community, and that they needed to learn from that experience.

I was stunned. I thought, *When is the last time that a foundation came out and said, "We have screwed over our community. We bulldozed a strategy into a community that harmed young people. Let's own our stuff."* It's unheard of. I had to give them a tiny bit of props for that. I could feel how my judgment of them eased up a little, and I was able to be more present. Immediately, a space had been opened for transformation and healing.

The next thing that struck me was how they reported the progress they had made on the problems around racial justice that had been identified during the first edition of that conference, one year prior. For example, the issue had been raised that the creators who were producing the content for Amazon Studios were not diverse enough. In the year since, Amazon had made a real effort, and now they were reporting back: "This is what it looked like, and this is what we did about it."

Again, I was amazed. The leadership had listened and responded. And again I thought about how rare that kind of listening and accountability is within the philanthropic sector. I go to conference after conference and read report after report, but all we do is talk about the changes we need to make. Then we move on. I appreciated that Amazon had identified a problem, created a strategy to address it, and made it happen in a short amount of time.

The final thing I witnessed that blew me away was an exercise in which a group of white men sat on the stage in a circle and had a conversation about their privileges as men and as white men, while around them, on the perimeter of the stage, was a second circle composed entirely of people of color. These men—who had been attending trainings about white privilege and patriarchy for some time, separately—sat on stage and had this public conversation with one another—often called the "fishbowl" exercise—and modeled holding each other accountable, while being witnessed by people of color. I got chills, I was so deeply moved.

When I spoke about it later with Angel Enriquez, a senior manager of diversity and inclusion at Amazon, she said they had wrestled with finding

> the right tension point between holding people accountable for educating themselves and not making it about their comfort, in a way that actually drives change. How can we hold that tension between challenging them and not making it so challenging that they just get overwhelmed and opt out? And then how do you create a space for them to take those new discoveries, that new feeling, and do something with it that is productive?[5]

Angel told me that they had discovered how important it was to find something in common, an intersection point, between two people with different identities, to create that human emotional connection, so they could hear each other. For example, perhaps a Black woman employee and a white male employee discover that they both are parents but have had a substantially different experience in talking to their kids about race. This can be an emotional learning moment for the white male employee, who, once confronted with considering race, is driven to understand his substantial privilege. This is the "sticky moment" that allows these two people to connect at a human level and to hear each other, which can be quickly followed up with specific actions and policies.

Again, I thought about how I'd never seen anything like it in other sectors, and how powerful it would be—what a burden it would take off the shoulders of folks of color—if white men organized themselves to hear and understand the issues and to hold each other accountable.

I think we sometimes forget that people are the system and the system is people. All our organizations and institutions, whether corporate, nonprofit, foundation, or government, are made up of people. Inside all of these places there are good people who speak up to push for change and to disrupt in that space. All we have to do is give them the floor and listen.

Relate

My favorite book as a child was *How to Win Friends and Influence People*, by Dale Carnegie. I've read it dozens of times, because I was clear at an early age that whatever I ended up doing in life would involve the world's most precious resource: people. We are all in the people business! In my experience, however, every institution and process that deals with money has this in common: a focus on transactions rather than relationships.

To prioritize relationship means that cultivating strong, authentic, caring human connection is valued over and above returns on investments and measurable results. It means recognizing that relationships, rather than the cash, are an institution's greatest asset, even for an institution that is focused on money. It means that those with wealth are not reduced to cash machines and those seeking funding are not reduced to gold diggers. There are real people hiding inside the business suits.

To create an atmosphere in which relationships come first, we need to start with the location and design of the space. No more ivory towers. If it's serious about connecting to the communities it serves, a foundation shouldn't be set off in the woods, surrounded by deer, with the offices occupying buildings that resemble plantations and the rooms filled with antiques that look like they belong to royal families. How can you serve disabled people if your rooms are not accessible to them? How can you serve transpeople if your restrooms are not welcoming to them? And why don't the windows in these places open, when the fields of philanthropy and finance so desperately need a breath of fresh air?

Banks and investment firms don't have to feel like they were carved from a block of ice, intimidating with their slick, angular surfaces and the long, rectangular tables with VIP seating on either end. Funders' offices don't have to look like yurts, either, though there's compelling evidence that spaces that encourage relationships have rounded edges and warm textiles, with the kitchen central. When people sit in circles, they feel like they're on more equal footing with one another. When people can cook and eat together, they connect on a human level. When people are physically comfortable, they are more likely to be themselves.

The influential architect and design theorist Christopher Alexander began critiquing contemporary architecture for creating lifeless, impersonal spaces way back in the mid-1970s, publishing a series of books in which he calls instead for structures that possess a quality of aliveness and wholeness, "beautiful places, places where you feel yourself, places where you feel alive."[1] These qualities impact the social interactions that can happen in those structures. As he writes elsewhere, "The structure of life I have described in buildings—the structure which I believe to be objective—is deeply and inextricably connected with the human person, and with the innermost nature of human feeling."[2] Certain kinds of spaces literally make people feel welcome, make visitors feel on equal footing with those already in the building, encourage people to interact and relate. Those are decolonized spaces.

"We have this belief that everything is about relationships," Pamela Shifman, the executive director of the NoVo Foundation at the time of our conversation, told me.

> So we actually spend almost no time on the written applications and we try to make things super easy. Often the best work is happening in places where people aren't writing the best applications about the work. That's also really true outside the U.S., like a million percent. We're also trying to have meetings not only at our office but to go to others. These things may seem small, but they create the opportunity for different kinds of conversations and relationships to emerge.
>
> It's good for both sides. As funders, we can tell when someone treats you as an ATM machine, just figuring how they're going to get the money out of me and don't see anything about me and who I am. So much shifts when we make space for real relationships. We really get to know each other and go deep. We share on a personal level. When you're with someone, you have to be able to really be with them. And know each other. And love each other. And to have real tension. You have to be able to disagree and even fight, and then say, "It's okay. We're still on the same team." I feel like we have to find ways to be able to develop meaningful relationships with people so that you actually can talk about what's actually going on and figure out how to move forward together.[3]

It's true that relationships are more complicated than transactions, as Pamela points out. There's a reason why folks vow to stick together "for better or for worse, for richer or for poorer, in sickness and in health." Real, complex relationships are necessary not only for whatever the present entails but also to face challenges in the future. Relationships create resilience; transactions don't.

Transactions are superficial. It's like the difference between dating and relating, in this day and age when dating apps are like marketplaces and you create profiles to sell yourself, to make yourself attractive to someone else. You're trying to pass a test, and at the same time you're judging someone else's presentation to see if they're good enough for you. Relating, on the other hand, is about authenticity and vulnerability. You let yourself be seen for who you are and you accept the other person for who they are. You allow the other person the benefit of the doubt. Mutual trust, respect, and appreciation deepen a relationship. We commit to supporting the success of the other person. We develop a sense that we are in this together.

A psychologist named Arthur Aron, who studies intimacy, developed a list of 36 questions, which became a viral sensation after appearing in the *New York Times* "Modern Love" column in 2015. The questions are designed to bring two strangers along the path of relationship, breaking down barriers gradually by revealing people's concerns, hopes, dreams, and secrets. Twenty-five questions in, after quite a bit of territory has been covered, each person is asked to make three true "we" statements that refer to the two of them together—in other words, at this point, they're in a relationship. Aron's 36 questions have been used in studies to explore cross-race relationships and prejudice; they've been used to reduce tensions between police officers and community members.[4] How great would it be if, alongside asking for your business plan and your unique proposition and your rate of return, funders asked the 36 questions, or at least a selection of them, until both sides could make three true "we" statements.

~~~~

There are a lot of vibrant conversations happening in the field of organizational design that explore what it looks like when an organization is structured horizontally, when the people who used to be powerless, at the bottom of the old pyramid model, are empowered and have a sense of agency. There are a lot of conversations about purpose-driven organizations and workplaces where the whole person is welcome.

Many industries and businesses have begun experimenting with moving toward open, participatory, and transparent processes. They are moving toward seeking and incorporating wisdom from all levels of the organization as well as from users or "the crowd." The functions of decision-making, goal setting, creation, implementation, and evaluation are being distributed among all these stakeholders as well, with the recognition that important insights and innovations come from those who previously were not included.

Many are exploring the benefits of sharing power, for example, in new forms of cooperative ownership or shareholding. The barriers between designer and consumer, expert and user are dissolving. There is more role fluidity. In the words of Jeremy Heimans and Henry Timms, who write about the distinction between "old power" and "new power": "New power operates differently, like a current. It is made by many; it is open, participatory, and peer-driven. It uploads and it shares. Like water or electricity, it's most forceful when it surges. The goal with new power is not to hoard it but to channel it."[5]

What if funders moved from hoarding resources and operating in obscurity to becoming transparent, accountable, and participatory? Rather than the formality of professionalism, it would rely on the wisdom of the community. Rather than dinosaur-style command-and-control methods that are based in scarcity and separation, funders would embrace abundance and trust.

What if the question became *How can everyone be powerful?* rather than *How can everyone have equal power?* In his book on organizational design, which adopts a framework of organization-as-organism rather than organization-as-machine, the Belgian scholar of human behavior and management Frederic Laloux writes, "People can hold different levels of power, and yet everyone can be powerful. . . . [As] in an ecosystem, interconnected organisms thrive without one holding power over another. . . . The point is not to make everyone equal; it is to allow all employees to grow into the strongest, healthiest version of themselves."[6]

In fact, what if funders no longer assumed that disadvantaged communities and individuals needed to be empowered at all? What if we acknowledged how powerful they inherently are? The irony of a project of empowerment is that it requires victims: if you need someone to give up power and make space for you, then you are a victim of the power dynamic. Transcending the drama triangle roles of perpetrator, victim, and savior involves everyone being allocated agency and responsibility.

We don't see a lot of these human-centered, horizontal, holistic models being adapted in the institutions along the loans-to-gifts spectrum, but there's no reason we can't start.

Represent

Effectively moving money to where the hurt is worst—using money as medicine—requires the funder to have deep, authentic knowledge of the issues and communities that will be putting the funding to use. Deep, authentic knowledge does not come from reading some stats, reports, or articles; it doesn't even come from a site visit to the affected community or interviewing someone from that community. It comes from living inside the community and experiencing that issue for oneself. Period.

Daryn Dodson's work through Illumen Capital is based on the psychology of racial biases and how people miss opportunities because of it, then applying that understanding to a financial framework. He notes:

> One of the things that was missing in terms of the overall sector of impact investing was the connection of entrepreneurs to the communities which they're trying to transform and create solutions for, or what Bryan Stevenson calls "proximity." So the idea that people who are investing large amounts of money to transform the world would

sit down with the communities that they're trying to transform is a really important pillar of what we're trying to accomplish.[1]

Bryan Stevenson, author of *Just Mercy* and the executive director of the Equal Justice Initiative, explains "proximity" as "Get close to the things that matter; get close to the places where there is inequality and suffering; get close to the spaces where people feel oppressed, burdened, and abused. See what it does to your capacity to make a difference; see what it does to you."[2]

This should not be a radical idea, people. In some sectors it's not. For example, in order to receive federal funds, 51 percent of a federally qualified health center's board has to be patients, which is to say, representatives of the people served. Yet among the majority of foundations, there's not a single person on staff—not to speak of the board—who possesses that lived experience and wisdom. Gara LaMarche, formerly of the Democracy Alliance, told me, "I think the most fundamental thing that philanthropies can do is democratize themselves, so that the decision-making is made by people the most affected. A more established way of doing that, which still people don't do enough, is to have boards that are really reflecting communities."[3]

The good news is that a handful of funders are already experimenting with collaboration and participation and representation. The Potlatch Fund in Seattle, created in 2004 with the sole focus of funding Native communities in the Northwest—one of the only foundations in the country giving 100 percent to Natives—has bylaws stipulating that two-thirds of the board seats be held by Native Americans. Their funding priorities are determined by talking circles in Native communities and are decided there, in the talking circles, based on consensus.

I spoke to Nevin Öztop who was working at FRIDA, a fund for young feminists in the Global South, which employs a participatory grantmaking process. FRIDA receives about 1,000 applicants per grantmaking cycle, who are then "invited to comment and vote on the 100 groups that they think should receive funding." The peer-review process promotes movement building in that it enhances critical analysis, connections, solidarity, and accountability among applicants. All of FRIDA's grants are awarded as flexible funds and core support, which allows groups to define their own budgets and to dedicate funds where they are most needed. In particular, FRIDA's grants can be used to cover traditionally and increasingly underfunded areas like overhead and general operating costs.

Nevin told me a story of one group who had applied, received one of the highest ratings from their peers, but then stepped back and offered their FRIDA grant to another group that they felt needed the money more. "I think the reason they did that was because they felt like it was their own money. There was an ownership of resources. They felt like they could decide on the fate of that money. We regranted it to another group that they thought should receive funding. It was such a nice moment."[4]

In the Australian state of Victoria, there was a fund called Towards a Just Society that had operated for 14 years as an offshoot of the Australian Communities Foundation, granting to Aboriginal people and communities in Victoria. In 2017–2018, they decided to transfer the fund to Indigenous control and engaged in a thoughtful and respectful transfer process to achieve this goal. In March 2019, the fund was launched as Koondee Woonga-gat Toor-rong—so named by Wurundjeri Elder, Aunty Diane Kerr. Koondee Woonga-gat Toor-rong means "to give jointly, to share together" in the Woiwurrung language. The first-ever Aboriginal and Torres Strait Islander–led fund in Victoria, it is evolving its own distinctive Indigenous grantmaking vision and practice, based around traditional cultural values and the principle of self-determination. As former executive officer John Harding says, philanthropy needs to be "less talking about us and more talking to us."[5]

Another potent example comes from the Brooklyn Community Foundation, which launched an initiative called Neighborhood Strength in the Crown Heights neighborhood in 2014. Neighborhood Strength positions the residents of the neighborhood as the key decision-makers for the foundation's investments. The foundation brought together more than 130 residents in three sessions in the fall of 2016 to identify their top concerns for the neighborhood and to propose solutions. Then 17 highly engaged residents came together to form an advisory council that reviewed those concerns and agreed on a focus, their one big idea: public space. The foundation set the terms of a request-for-proposals process based on the advisory council's recommendation. When the proposals came in, the advisory council selected the winning projects.[6]

These are all great steps forward toward real representation, from some of the most progressive funders out there. A participatory model has also been attempted in municipalities around the world and was even experimented with by the White House: it's called participatory budgeting. In Porto Alegre, Brazil, where the idea was born some 25 years ago, as many as 50,000 residents vote on how to spend public money each year. New York and Boston have experimented with it. And under the Obama administration, participatory budgeting became an option for determining how to spend community development block grant money from the Department of Housing and Urban Development.[7]

Granted, the model risks reinforcing white privilege and class privilege, since currently more white middle- and upper-class voters vote in participatory budgeting processes, but it doesn't have to be that way. In 2013, in Chicago, one councilman (Joe Moore, of the 49th Ward) took the $1.3 million "menu money," which the city gives to each of the 50 councilmembers to use for capital improvements, and opened up the allocation process to his community. People starting at age 16 (younger than in a regular election), both residents and citizens, were invited to vote on the menu money.[8] In the case of that Chicago ward, a clear intention and outreach made the process more truly democratic and representative of the population.

~~~

In order for us to decolonize wealth, at least half of the people who make the decisions about where money goes—at least 50 percent of staff, 50 percent of advisors, 50 percent of board members—should have intimate, authentic knowledge of the issues and communities involved. This means that some of the usual suspects, the white saviors, will have to give up their seats. They'll have to step back, rather than just making a token seat open next to them. This will definitely require an attitude adjustment for some. As Jordan Flaherty writes in his book on the savior complex, "For people born into privilege, decentering yourself can feel difficult. It involves giving up a certain amount of privilege."[9] And as the saying goes, when you're accustomed to privilege, equality feels like oppression. That discomfort is part of the healing.

As Paulina Helm Hernandez, a queer Latina organizer and artist, former codirector of Southerners on New Ground (SONG), and now a program officer at the Foundation for a Just Society, said to white people wanting to be allies to people of color, "You don't have to always be the final vote on the strategy, pace, timing, tone and approach. Put another way, it means you have to learn how to share political imagination, power, and work without having to always be in charge. . . . You have to be willing to trust leaders of color who have the track record, integrity, and vision to get things done."[10]

In 2017, for the first time in its history, the Andrus Family Fund invited three community board members to join its board of directors, including yours truly. We were full-fledged trustees, with the same rights and votes as the family board members; in fact, one, a Black woman, became the board chair in 2019. The fund had never previously included nonfamily members on the board, so when they decided to open seats to the community, they opened up three seats simultaneously, rather than starting with a single, token seat. There's some research indicating that when integrating new people into an existing culture or structure, you want to shoot for the newbies being 30 percent of the total, or, at a minimum, three people.[11]

AFF's strategy reflected their commitment to the foundation authentically representing what will soon be the new American majority. Inviting community board members to join was a natural extension of AFF's social justice values, yet getting to this place of shared power required more than eight years of deep discussion and deliberation before making the jump. Family members on the board revealed to me that the biggest obstacle was their fear of being judged, since it was only because they were family that they were on the board in the first place.

What if foundations had to apply for the honor of funding communities and projects, rather than the other way around? Phillip Jackson dedicated his life to improving the lives of Black Chicagoans. When he founded the Black Star Project—which provides mentoring, tutoring, parental engagement, politics exposure, career development, and violence prevention—he intentionally built into the organization a business model with multiple funding streams, only minimally supported by foundations. This meant, as Phillip put it:

> We're able to hold people more accountable who other people dare not hold accountable. . . . Most not-for-profits have a subservient relationship with foundations. That's not something we were willing to be. When we were coming to the foundation, we were saying, "Hey, you need us as much as we need you." That's not something the foundations were used to hearing, but that was our attitude. Our attitude was "Look, there are problems out there. These problems need solutions. We have solutions; you have dollars to fund the solutions. Let's work together."[12]

As I wrote in my tribute to Phillip Jackson in April 2019, after I learned of his passing, his boldness created space for people like me to continue pushing for inclusion and progress.

Those who are truly intentional about the work of healing from decolonization understand that representation of people of color alone is not sufficient—the outcome is simply token diversity. We must go beyond representation to sharing ownership and full inclusion.

STEP SIX

Invest

When people learn that the same company that is selling a cure is simultaneously contributing to the cause of the disease, they get mad, and understandably so. There was a huge uproar around 2002 when activists revealed this was exactly what was happening with the pink ribbon breast cancer fundraising campaign. Cosmetics companies that were simultaneously using breast-cancer-linked chemicals in their products were "pinkwashing"—enticing consumers with the assurance that they were contributing a portion of their proceeds to fight the disease. I'm sorry to say that this dynamic is taking place in the very heart of philanthropy and ethical investing. And it needs to stop.

Since 1969, U.S. tax law has mandated that foundations pay out a *minimum* of 5 percent of their total assets each year in the form of grants or eligible administration expenses. The "payout rule" was created to prevent foundations from receiving assets but never actually making charitable distributions with them. The other 95 percent of the assets are invested with the goal of earning financial returns that sustain the grantmaking power of the foundation over time. It makes zero sense that a foundation that aims to stop global warming with the 5 percent it pays out would simultaneously invest its assets in fossil fuel industries, right? Yet this kind of contradiction occurs all the time. This is unconscionable.

What about the 95 percent? This is a question all of us need to be asking, and almost no one is. It's only just in recent years, after a decade in the field, that I've awakened to the 95 percent. What is going on with that money? For those of us in the field, it's as if there's a firewall. We're kept in the dark about what's happening on the other side. We're not privy to conversations about the corpus, yet that's where the real power is, because it's where the vast, vast majority of the money is working. The 5 percent we're in charge of allocating is just a drop in the bucket.

At one of the foundations where I worked, we would have a quarterly ice cream party to celebrate when our investments paid off, increasing our corpus. This puzzled me. *Weren't higher levels of giving what we were supposed to be celebrating?* During my interview with Dana Arviso, the former executive director of the Potlatch Fund, we spoke about the backwardness of the priorities. I began, "In philanthropy, we ask how big you are, which foundation has the largest amount of assets in the bank—"

Dana jumped in, finishing my thought: "That's where your prestige and your status comes from, rather than how much you give away."

The Potlatch Fund is named for the potlatch ceremonies common among the tribes of the Pacific Northwest, who had such an abundance of natural resources that they began a practice of ceremonially giving it all away— redistributing wealth. "The status of certain chiefs here in the Northwest was measured by how many potlatches they had in their lifetime," Dana told me. "Some of the most esteemed chiefs in the Northwest had six or seven potlatches in their lifetime. We're talking about gathering up everything that they had and giving it all away, for the purpose of creating strong relationships with neighboring tribal communities."[1]

Most foundations don't even disclose information about their investments. Fewer than half of the 15 biggest U.S. foundations, which together own tens of billions of dollars in assets, report on their investments.[2]

Meanwhile, investors who tout the "Doing well by doing good" mantra—whether they call it ethical investing, socially responsible investing, impact investing, or even microlending—are all too often playing the same game. A portion of their investments may be going to fund solar-powered lamps and clean cookstoves for poor Africans, but at the same time the majority of their money is "safely" invested in traditional places where a solid return is expected, and that might well mean in mining companies that are destroying the soil and groundwater of those same poor Africans.

It's true that divestment campaigns have been fairly effective at shining the light on these kinds of hypocrisies and inconsistencies with regard to specific issues, most famously with the apartheid regime in South Africa in the 1980s, with fossil fuels over the past decade, and most recently with divestment from banks that supported the Dakota Access Pipeline. The opposite of investment, divestment campaigns put pressure on investors to get rid of stocks, bonds, or investment funds that are supporting an unhealthy, unethical, or downright evil activity. Divestment activists have successfully demanded that municipalities, universities and colleges, religious organizations, retirement funds, and other institutions stop funding the bad stuff. As we saw with the South African divestment campaign, it can really work. By the mid-1980s, 22 countries, 90 cities, and 155 campuses had pulled their funding from companies that did business in South Africa, which contributed to the end of the apartheid government.[3]

But why should philanthropy and ethical investment have to rely on whistle-blowers and independent activists to keep the bulk of their assets from causing harm? Those assets should be both transparent and 100 percent aligned with the mission of the foundation. This is known as mission-related investing. The concept has already found support among many of the big players in philanthropy, including the Kellogg Foundation, the John D. and Catherine T. MacArthur Foundation, the Bill and Melinda Gates Foundation, and Open Society Foundations. In April 2017, the president of the Ford Foundation, Darren Walker, announced that Ford was embracing it as well:

> I am pleased that after many months of analysis and planning, the Ford Foundation's Board of Trustees has authorized the allocation of up to $1 billion of our endowment, to be phased in over 10 years, for mission-related investments. Since the 1980s, divestment movements around the world have asked institutional investors, in particular, to consider how their investments are related to the wider world. Whether they were demanding divestment from tobacco, fossil fuels, or apartheid South Africa, these movements reminded us that our investments are part of a broad ecosystem of consequences, intended and unintended—consequences that we realized we could not ignore. Today, we have an opportunity to build on this proud, powerful legacy. Previous

divestment movements tried to prevent investors from harming society; now, institutional investors can begin to move from "do no harm" to exploring how to "do more good."[4]

The move received a lot of positive attention and will likely inspire other foundations to follow suit, which is definitely positive. But here's the thing: Ford's total endowment is more than $12 billion. So this move doesn't even impact 10 percent of their assets. Darren Walker acknowledged it's just the start; it's not enough to move the dial.

We need to move the dial, people. The F.B. Heron Foundation provides an excellent model to follow. Founded in 1992 with the mission of helping people and communities to move out of poverty and thrive, by 1996 the board began considering what could be done with the 95 percent, realizing that a "foundation should be more than a private investment company that uses its excess cash flow for charitable purposes." Within a decade, Heron's mission-related activity had grown to comprise approximately 40 percent of its overall endowment and included everything from taxable municipal bonds to private equity. In 2012, they decided to go from 40 percent to 100 percent mission-related investments. However, they quickly discovered that there were relatively few truly mission-aligned, poverty-oriented investment managers out there in the market. Instead, there were a growing number of impact-screened vehicles. By December 21, 2016, Heron moved the last unscreened piece of its corpus to impact-screened exchange-traded funds; up next, they'll be pushing their portfolio from screened-for-impact to invested-for-mission.[5]

Another foundation that's leading the way is the McConnell Foundation in Canada. When I spoke with

McConnell's president and CEO, Stephen Huddart, he told me about several exciting things they're doing with their endowment:

> We make intentional use of our endowment to build financial products and investments that are in line with our philanthropic mission. For close to seven years we've been funding an Indigenous social innovation lab in Winnipeg, Manitoba, working out of Canada's poorest, urban neighborhood. The Province of Manitoba apprehends more than ten thousand kids who are put into state care, with ninety percent of them Indigenous kids. The social innovation lab developed a model for an Indigenous doula program to hire and train women to accompany mothers through their pregnancy, birth, and first few months of raising a child, in a culturally appropriate way and with a view to weaving together community support, to ensure that mothers were off to a good start and thereby reducing the number of children who are apprehended. The doula program is now a three million–dollar social impact bond project where the government is backstopping investments or grants by a group of foundations and investors in taking this model to scale.
>
> We've been very careful to make it clear that we don't want a financial return from our investment and we'll happily have a zero return or a minus-five-percent return, and we'll donate to the initiative any financial return that might otherwise be due to us and encourage that as a model of integrating granting with investment. So we're

able to do something at a scale that we couldn't as a foundation on our own. It's a promising example of how we can co-invest with the idea of creating better outcomes for children and families with a community-led and community-enabling structure.

We've also been very involved in supporting Canada's first Indigenous venture capital fund, Raven Capital Partners, which directs capital to Indigenous entrepreneurs. We've worked with this group to develop something called the Community Directed Outcomes Contract, a financial innovation—a little bit like a social impact bond, except that it's community-determined. The priority is set by the community and then investors and an outcome buyer are able to put capital to work. The first deal they've done involves removing diesel generator systems which rely on imported diesel fuel for powering the community with geothermal solar, renewable energy, and creating local jobs in that process. So it's not contractors being flown in to do the job and then leave. It's training local people to do the work and keep doing it and become part of an Indigenous-owned enterprise, the community involved at every step of the way.

We also have a business partnership with the Huron in Quebec, who have a model for creating owned housing on reservations, which is usually impossible because those lands are held by the Crown. The Huron have found a workaround for this: basically setting up community-run mortgage funds so that people can have access to

capital, and therefore the ability to build equity in
a house. You have equity, you can borrow against
that, and people are now able to get business loans
and use equity like anybody else, like people in
non-Indigenous or mainstream society have been
able to do for a long time. We're working together
to scale up this model so that it's moving through
other reservations in Quebec and in Northern BC
and the Yukon.[6]

And what about risks and returns? Ford's relatively
cautious $1 billion over 10 years reflects a fear of "under-
performance," as they say in finance language, meaning
there's a lower rate of profit. This is sacrilege to many
investment committees of foundations, who insist on protecting the endowment for perpetuity. Heron's investment
policy statement makes its stance clear:

> For Heron, return is measured both in financial
> terms and by the degree to which any given use
> of capital leads to outcomes that are consistent
> with our philanthropic mission and public pur-
> pose. In this policy statement, "risk" refers to the
> probability of non-performance on both social
> and financial dimensions, and on the interaction
> between the two. . . . We believe that investments
> in targeted enterprises with positive net contri-
> bution will perpetuate a cycle of favorable social
> performance, financial performance, and ulti-
> mately financial return.[7]

There are also those who say that the widespread fear
of diminished financial returns is bogus. Kristin Hull, an
impact investor and advisor based in the San Francisco

Bay Area, decided to go 100 percent mission-invested back in 2007, when she moved all the assets of her family foundation out of the market and into seven local community banks. By 2008, when the recession hit, foundation endowments nationwide were down by 28 percent, but her family's was up by 2 percent. Since then, her investment philosophy has gotten even sharper: "I just can't invest in any more white men unless they're part of a diverse team. They're already getting the money. Knowing that women receive less than 4 percent of venture capital and people of color just 1 percent, that is the most meaningful and impactful place for me to invest."[8]

Kristin's women-and-people-of-color-only screen for investments is the necessary next step for all of us. It's not enough to just not allow the bulk of our assets to fund the bad stuff; we have to take those assets and invest in the more beautiful world our hearts know is possible. If you believe, as I do, that the best solutions to the current economic and social problems are coming from the very people who were disempowered by the colonial command-and-control, dominate-and-exploit system, then those are the people in whom we need to invest.

Corporations can get in on this, too, and use their equity in the same way foundations can use their endowments. We saw a great example of this from Netflix as a response to the resurgence of the Black Lives Matter movement after the murder of George Floyd. On June 30, 2020, the chief financial officer of Netflix announced they were allocating 2 percent of their cash holdings—initially up to $100 million—to financial institutions and organizations that directly support Black communities in the United States. Other corporate leaders contacted them after the announcement to find out how they could do the same, and on June 24 Netflix offered a coaching session to support them in following suit. This fired up Tracy Nowski, a partner at the global consulting firm McKinsey, to invite 30 CFOs from McKinsey's large corporate clients to join the session and encourage them to make the same move.

My colleague Vanessa Daniel, executive director of the Groundswell Fund, has written that philanthropy's efforts will have gone far enough in this direction

> when the majority of foundations acknowledge the fact that white supremacy is in fact blocking progress on everything their trustees care about, and that they have little hope of advancing their missions, whether finding cures for cancer, ending malaria, improving STEM [science, technology, engineering, and mathematics] education, promoting the arts, or protecting fragile ecosystems, if they don't fund work that recognizes and dismantles white supremacy.[9]

So, to repeat: there needs to be total transparency around where our assets are invested, and those assets must be 100 percent mission-aligned—meaning not just doing no harm but also actively invested in decolonization—in order to heal divides and restore balance.

STEP SEVEN

Repair

Recent numbers indicate that global foundation assets have topped $1.5 trillion.[1] Collectively, America's foundations have about $900 billion in assets. PwC anticipates that global assets under management will almost double in size by 2025, from $84.9 trillion in 2016 to $111.2 trillion by 2020, and then again to $145.4 trillion by 2025.[2] That's a lot of wealth, and it is wealth that was made on the backs of Natives and African Americans and low-wage workers, following the directives of colonization: *divide, control, exploit*. Our peoples and our lands were exploited over generations, over centuries, and this is ongoing.

Yet despite our role in creating that wealth, white supremacy continues to deny us access to it. We are demeaned for our lack of resources and are called lazy. We must jump through hoops and prove ourselves worthy to get a piece of it in the form of loans or grants. As I've shown, of the fairly insignificant 5 percent that is annually paid out of those $900 billion held by foundations, the little bit of funding specifically earmarked to support people of color has actually been shrinking.[3]

Phillip Jackson, founder of Black Star Project in Chicago, had some stern words for foundations: "These guys will lean back in their ivory towers, in their luxury corporate suites, while the blood of Black children is running in the streets of Chicago. I told them, 'You guys are something! You're funding classical music; you're funding impressionistic art . . . and Black children are dying right down the street from right where you are.'"⁴ He analyzed the grantmaking of the MacArthur Foundation, the largest funder in Chicago, using the information from the foundation's own website. "They have $7 billion in assets and follow the 5 percent payout rule." He characterized the $375,000 in funds given to Black-led, Black-serving organizations, out of the total $56 **million** in grants given to Chicago organizations by the MacArthur Foundation, as "modern-day redlining."⁵

Jackson led a legendary "one-man crusade" to make MacArthur pay attention to the community where it was based. Due to his untimely passing in November 2018, shortly after the first edition of this book was released, I never had the chance to meet this courageous truth teller in person. After publishing a tribute to him when I learned of his death, I did have the chance to meet his sister, and I later received this message from his colleague Cheryl Heads:

> Phillip not only caught MacArthur off guard, but put other large foundations on notice. Funding to communities of color in Chicago has increased substantially since then. I had POC [people of color]-led organizations say to me (off the record, of course) that they knew the grants they received from MacArthur and other foundations were directly related to Phillip's protest. Remarkably, although other POC-led

organizations benefited from his actions, Phillip did not. There was and remains to this day a huge backlash against his organization for his speaking out. You mentioned in your book that this should not have been his responsibility to take on the fight alone. However, Phillip was fully aware of what the consequences would be, and he knew he had to take action anyway.[6]

Indeed, there is no question that Phillip Jackson was a brave and tireless hero, and yet we shouldn't have to count on community members being so fearless. The commitment to repair should come from the side with the wealth and the power it confers.

As I've noted, loans, venture capital, municipal bonds, and other investments are also smaller in size, harder to get, and often are of poorer quality or higher risk when they go to people of color. And despite the evolution of ethical finance or impact finance, just one of every five dollars under professional financial management is invested according to socially responsible strategies,[7] and there is likewise no guarantee that people of color will gain access to it.

Since the wealth was extracted from our resources and our work, it is understandable that we're a little frustrated and impatient with institutions of wealth that evaluate our worthiness and risk potential as recipients and then give crumbs.

Reparations are due.

Using money as medicine in its most powerful, direct form means we use it to heal the racial wealth gap. Decolonizing wealth is, at its essence, about closing the racial wealth gap. Poverty is the product of public policy and theft, facilitated by white supremacy.

There's an important distinction being made in the new conversations about reparations. We're not just talking about making up for the crimes of the past, for the near genocide of Native Americans 500 or 200 years ago, when the settlers first arrived and spread over the land, or for the slave trade and slavery. We're talking about layers and layers of trauma caused by white supremacist exploitation. We're talking about Jim Crow. We're talking about the exclusions built into the New Deal that disadvantaged people of color by not counting certain professions (such as farming and domestic work) as worthy of benefits. We're talking about white boarding schools that ripped Native American families apart and stamped out the surviving culture less than a hundred years ago under the motto "Kill the Indian, Save the Man." We're talking about how the benefits of the G.I. Bill were racialized. We're talking about redlining practices. We're talking about the elite universities of this country being built with profits from slavery and how students and faculty of color still feel excluded today. We're talking about the criminal justice system's hugely disproportionate impact on communities of color. We're talking about Native Americans' unemployment rates being 10 times the national average. We're talking about immigration policies dividing parents from their children right now. We're talking about the violence and exploitation that have impacted four out of five Native women. We're talking about the images in the media that constantly criminalize people of color. We're talking about the lack of police accountability for the killing of unarmed Native and Black men and women. We're talking about the inequality in bank loans and venture capital that impact people of color. Above all, we're talking about how all these—and many other events and policies and cultural practices—have worked together to keep wealth and well-being disproportionately concentrated in white communities.

As Richard F. America of Georgetown University has said, "We want to correct a current, not a past, injustice. The current injustice is that the top 30 percent of the income distribution, overwhelmingly White, enjoys this $5 to $10 trillion unjust enrichment."[8] The writer Ta-Nehisi Coates has also written eloquently on the subject of reparations:

> The wealth gap merely puts a number on something we feel but cannot say—that American prosperity was ill-gotten and selective in its distribution. What is needed is an airing of family secrets, a settling with old ghosts. What is needed is a healing of the American psyche and the banishment of white guilt. What I'm talking about is more than recompense for past injustices—more than a handout, a payoff, hush money, or a reluctant bribe. What I'm talking about is a national reckoning that would lead to spiritual renewal.[9]

So what could the institutions along the loans-to-gifts spectrum do to make and support reparations, in concrete terms?

Philanthropy, as the sector most ostensibly responsible for healing, could and should lead the way. The institutions of philanthropy as a whole could take 10 percent of their assets—10 percent tithed from each foundation in existence—and establish a trust fund to which Native Americans and African Americans could apply for grants for various asset-building projects, such as home ownership, further education, or startup funds for businesses. This reparations tithing among foundations could happen right now, without legislation, as a demonstration of commitment from the philanthropic community. No specifications around how that money is spent; no reporting. No strings attached. Right now.

I offered this challenge to philanthropy in the first edition of this book, but I doubted that any foundations would take me up on it and hand over 10 percent of their assets to communities of color and Indigenous people as a way to jump-start reparations. Imagine my surprise when I encountered a foundation that was leading the way! The McConnell Foundation is a private foundation in Canada that came to the realization that their founder originally benefited from Indigenous lands and resources, as part of the colonial history there, and so they decided to give a chunk back. McConnell mobilized five or six other foundations, all of whom made significant contributions (although not quite 10 percent of their assets . . . yet), to set up an Indigenous-led foundation called the Indigenous Resilience Fund.[10]

I spoke with Stephen Huddart, McConnell's president and CEO, about this. "Although funders were giving to Indigenous communities, there was nothing that Indigenous people were actually running themselves, managing and directing the funds," he told me. "We see this as being a sizeable foundation in Canada, to which we will be inviting *all* foundations to contribute a portion of their endowments." When I pressed him on the specific 10 percent of assets vision, he admitted that they weren't there yet, but he said, "People are discussing it and recognizing that it definitely should be part of our future and would be the right thing to do. This is a way to pay back or to make a more than symbolic contribution to restitution."[11]

Another funder inspired by the book is the St. Paul–based Bush Foundation, which makes grants in Minnesota,

North and South Dakota, and the 23 Native nations that share that geography. In the fall of 2019, their board approved a process to finance the equivalent of roughly 10 percent of their endowment to create a community trust fund for Native and Black folks in the region—committing $100 million in direct payments to individuals to support efforts like home ownership, education, and entrepreneurship. Obviously, this approach does not take the place of formal reparations, but it is a fantastic step forward to help address the profound racial wealth gaps that both reflect historic injustice and are a root cause of so many ongoing racial disparities.

Another idea might be to replace traditional funding mechanisms with the living resource system approach outlined by folks at Movement Net Lab:

> A living resource system provides a relationship-based approach to resources: resources are identified, linked, moved, supported, and restructured by everyone in the network so that they fit the dynamic nature of networked movements. Resources need to be placed in funding pools where activists can be central to the decision-making process, and funds need to be structured so they can flow to the emerging landscape of self-organized actions rather than just through formal, pre-existing organizations. . . . Funders can have much greater impact if they know how to support with greater precision at each moment, shifting and adapting in real time as the moment evolves.[12]

As early examples of the model, they mention Occupy Sandy, where folks set up Amazon wedding registries that identified needed items that supporters anywhere on earth could purchase to be delivered directly to sites hit by Hurricane Sandy, and the Accomplices on Demand network, made up of non-Black people in the Boston area who support Black people's dignity by making their resources, skills, and Rolodexes available, and by engaging in antiracist conversations with people who look like them.

Philanthropy and social and ethical finance also could lead the charge in establishing the foundation for what Professor William A. Darity Jr. of Duke University has called the "Baby Bonds proposal"—although he's actually not talking about a bond; it's more like a trust fund. It would be a publicly provided trust fund given to each newborn child, but the amount of the fund would vary based on the wealth of the child's family. Bill Gates's baby might get $50, Darity has suggested, while the baby of the lowest-income family might get something in the thousands or tens of thousands. This would involve no race-based or heritage-based eligibility but would obviously address the wealth gap for the upcoming and future generations.[13]

A true commitment to this plan from the finance sector could come in the form of the financial transaction tax. This minuscule fee charged on the trading of stocks, currencies, debt instruments (like bonds and treasury notes), and derivatives (futures and options) would hardly be felt by investors. An FTT of 0.25 percent—$1 on every $400 of stock traded—would generate hundreds of billions of dollars. Only the top 10 percent of American households own more than $20,000 in stocks directly (as opposed to their pensions, for instance, being invested in the market), so it would be this most affluent community for whom the tax on trading activity would even be perceptible. Even a more conservative rate of tax, such as what was proposed in the Inclusive Prosperity Act introduced in the U.S. House of Representatives in 2012 and the U.S. Senate in 2015 (0.5 percent for all stock transactions, 0.1 percent for all bond transactions, and 0.005 percent on the notional value of all derivative trades), would still generate $220 billion per year, according to researchers.[14]

With a handsome sum like $220 billion, we could also look at funding broad social programs such as free universal health care or free universal college education, which, as the Movement for Black Lives has suggested, would disproportionately benefit African Americans and could be part of a reparations portfolio. We could also take a chunk of that money and buy land for Natives—land to which we actually have full property rights. (Reservations are held "in trust" by the federal government. The economist Hernando de Soto has called it "dead capital" because we can't put it to use by selling it, buying more to take advantage of economies of scale, or borrowing against it.)[15]

The conversation around reparations has advanced since the first edition of this book was released in 2018. For example, a number of colleges and universities have publicly acknowledged that they were built by enslaved workers and upheld the system of white supremacy. In 2019, Harvard University launched an initiative "to understand and address the enduring legacy of slavery within our university."[16] The Virginia Theological Seminary announced a $1.7 million reparations fund to be used to aid the descendants of the enslaved workers who built its campus, and of those who lived in the community during the Jim Crow era, when "the seminary participated in that unjust and racist regime."[17]

A 2019 survey of all the Democratic presidential candidates on the issue of reparations found that all but one—Michael Bloomberg—voiced support for some form of reparations and the need to formally study the options. By contrast, in 2016 neither Barack Obama nor Hillary Clinton was willing to voice their support of reparations.[18] In a statement to the *Washington Post*, President Joe Biden made an unmistakable commitment:

> We must acknowledge that there can be no realization of the American dream without grappling with the original sin of slavery, and the centuries-long campaign of violence, fear, and trauma wrought upon Black people in this country. As president, I will immediately take action to address the systemic racism that is persistent across our institutions today. . . . That's why I have developed education, climate change and health-care policies, among others, that will root out this systemic racism and ensure that all Americans have a fair shot at living the American dream. While my administration takes major actions to address systemic racism, it will also study how reparations may be part of those efforts and ensure the voices of descendants are central when gathering data and information.[19]

The year 2020 also saw some ancestral lands being restored to Native hands. The Supreme Court ruled that 3 million acres of Oklahoma remains reservation lands.[20] Forty acres of land in Central California's Inyo County were returned to the Lone Pine Paiute–Shoshone people,[21] and the Esselen Tribe of Monterey County recovered 1,199 acres, supported by a $4.5 million grant from the California Natural Resources Agency that covered the purchase price of the property.[22]

In his book *From Here to Equality*, coauthored with his wife, Kirsten Mullen, Professor Darity states that a reparations program should accomplish three things in order to provide healing: acknowledgment, restitution, and closure. As he describes it:

> *Acknowledgement* involves the recognition on the part of the beneficiaries of the social injustice that's in question; an acknowledgement on the part of the beneficiaries of that social injustice that there has been a wrong committed and that there must be some form of repair to be provided to the folks who are the victims of that injustice. *Restitution* constitutes the actual program that's enacted to undertake that form of repair. *Closure* constitutes the acknowledgement on the part of the victimized community that they have received a satisfactory act of compensation from the victimizers, and that they have no reason to request anything that's specifically for their group in the future, unless there's a new wave of injustices.[23]

In September of 2019, I launched Liberated Capital, a fund to support healing and liberation primarily for Indigenous and Black folks. Rooted in relationships of mutuality and equity, Liberated Capital moves money through a reparations model. We used the structure of a donor-advised fund to move money out quickly, but unlike many donor-advised funds, we operate transparently, relying on the direction of Indigenous and Black leaders. I like to call it trust-based, untethered funding, rejecting traditional reporting models to be able to respond to community needs in real time. Rather than keeping funders distant, in their bubble of similarly endowed peers, Liberated Capital creates a community, an experience, and a commitment to a process of healing. We build bridges between individuals with wealth and communities that have been harmed by how that wealth was accumulated. Black, Indigenous, and other people of color are centered in a reparations journey with white wealthy individuals.

With this model, we created a COVID-19 rapid response initiative for hard-hit Indigenous communities. By December 2020, the fund had disbursed more than $1 million to Native-led organizations, which benefited more than 500,000 people in Native communities across the country. The fund supported the purchase and delivery of food, water, and other basic necessities such as masks, sanitizers, and diapers; facilitated virtual spaces for healing; offered direct services to victims of domestic violence; provided child-care services for essential workers; directly provided financial support to those unable to pay rent and utility bills; and provided emergency housing assistance. In the wake of the murder of George Floyd and the subsequent uprising for justice, we were also able to support Black-led groups in their efforts for liberation and healing.

In addition, I launched a direct cash program for Native Americans impacted by the pandemic. At the close of 2020, we had given more than $1 million in direct cash payments to 2,000 Native American families in a targeted, national program to provide mutual aid to individuals impacted by the crisis in North Carolina, Oklahoma, South Dakota, Alaska, and among the Hopi Tribe in Arizona. The program launch came amid the failure of the federal government to distribute millions of dollars in funds that were promised to Native American tribes as part of the CARES Act.[24] The direct cash model puts trust in the hands of recipients, allowing them to determine what their needs are, and provides a cushion of financial support that government programs have failed to provide. In addition to the loss of life, tribes lost an estimated $4.4 billion in economic activity and $997 million in wages, which exacerbates existing economic disparities facing Native Americans.[25]

Liberated Capital aims to be a transformational process that incorporates the Seven Steps to Healing: grieve, apologize, listen, relate, represent, invest, and repair. First, we recognize the pain that the accumulation of wealth has caused, and how this wealth was made on the backs of Indigenous people, slaves, and low-wage workers of color. We reopen these wounds, grieve them, and apologize. We listen to each other. We walk our talk about diversity and equity, ensuring our decision-making is directed by Indigenous people and other people of color. Finally, we use our money to heal where people are hurting, and to stop more hurt from happening.

It's the most powerful commitment that can be made to decolonizing wealth and healing our country. Reparations are the ultimate way to build power in exploited communities. They are the ultimate way to use money as medicine. The institutions of philanthropy and finance can take a giant leap forward and make a commitment, leading the way for government to finally follow suit.

What if foundations, banks, investors, and other institutions controlling wealth could imagine they had no history and no legacy? What if we imagined it was Day 1 and our mission is to build the best organization and the best model to achieve everyone's well-being? What if we could be unencumbered by "the way it's done" and liberated to design ourselves from scratch? What if we could use money as medicine? What if we could liberate money to be used as a tool of love?

Yeah, but what if we could?

CONCLUSION

Coming Full Circle

Decolonization takes us deep into the serpent's belly to confront the white supremacy, the savior complex, and the internalized oppression that are entrenched in ourselves, our institutions, and our society. Only then can we heal from the trauma of the separation worldview that divided the world into Us versus Them and led to exploitation, fear, and suffering.

As we emerge from that process, however long it may require, we're able to step into the role of becoming healers. The opportunities for healing, for finding medicine in our daily lives—whether in our families, in our workplaces, or in the institutions we support or belong to—start appearing everywhere. The medicine that calls us to use it in service of healing might be our own stories, our money, our possessions, our company, or our land. Every day offers new possibilities for healing, on smaller and larger scales. As we grow more confident in our identities as healers and in using the Seven Steps to Healing, we can contemplate change at the largest scale: not just institutions but systems. We can lay a new social, cultural, and economic foundation based on new ways of relating to each other and to our resources. This is what it is to come full circle.

With its focus on connection and belonging, the Indigenous worldview—having persisted against all odds, like Indigenous people themselves—offers inspiration for the way forward.

~~~

The state motto of my home state of North Carolina is "Esse quam videri," a Latin phrase meaning "To be, rather than to seem." It was also my mother's motto in child-rearing. I can hear her now: "No half-stepping! We must be *real* Christians, not just in name. We must *really* love people, not just do good for how it looks."

As it turns out, looking back, the first actual philanthropist I ever knew was my mother, not that she would have ever used that word. After nearly a decade and a half of my working in the field, when she is asked what I do, she will say "philanthropy," but she still stumbles over the word, and I'd be willing to bet that she couldn't spell it. Can we agree that words in English made of Greek roots were created so we'd have no idea what doctors are saying? So they can charge lots of money when they diagnose you with *hypergargalesthesia*? Yes, that's a real condition: extreme sensitivity to tickling.

But I use the word "philanthropy" because if you go by the Greek roots, philanthropy is about the love (*phil*) of humanity (*anthropos*).

To enable me to have a better life, my mom—a single mother—worked two or three shifts a day for most of my childhood. Two of those shifts were as a domestic worker, providing nursing assistance, helping sick, frail, and elderly (mostly wealthy) folks. A labor of love. Her first shift was at the Department of Motor Vehicles, a nine-to-five. Then she went to work providing care in a nursing home or someone's home for her second shift. And then came a third shift at someone's home, where, if she was lucky, she could get a few hours of sleep amid caretaking, until the shift ended at seven a.m., when she'd come home, change clothes, and start all over again. I'd tag along as often as possible. Many nights I hid in the car until the previous nurse left, then she'd sneak me into the houses, where I would play the grand pianos, read in the libraries (this is where I discovered *How to Win Friends and Influence People*), and then get tucked into beds or couches.

On her precious days off, did the poor woman put her feet up and eat bonbons? No, she did outreach for church. She helped start a bus ministry. This involved not just her Sundays but her Saturdays, too. Actually, *our* Saturdays, because I went along. If I was lucky, we'd stop at Bojangles and grab a cinnamon biscuit first, for sustenance. For years, we spent Saturdays going from neighborhood to neighborhood, knocking on doors, saying some variation of "Hi, I'm Sheila from the neighborhood. We go to this church and we just want to invite you to come attend sometime. If you have kids, we have a bus that is more than happy to come by and pick them up for Sunday school."

On Sunday mornings, when we went to get them, the bus would pull up and most times I was the person to jump out, run up, and knock on the door. "I'm here to pick up Tasha" (or whoever). Standing there at the door, waiting for the kid to come out, I saw a lot of bad things that made me grateful. Although my mom and I were poor, there were people who were much poorer, more troubled. Kids were pushed to the door looking a mess, unwashed, half-dressed. Or I'd get sent in to fetch them—"They're in the back room. Go get them."—and I'd have to climb over a man passed out from drink, surrounded by beer cans.

My mom was passionate about getting kids to church, and the bus ministry program grew to 300 children in our small community—300 children getting bused in to attend our church. To this day, children—now grown children—come running up and hug my mom, shouting, "Sister Sheila, Sister Sheila! You probably don't remember me, but you used to pick me up on a bus and oh my God, you were so special to me."

Most of those kids were just so hungry for love. They'd be trying to climb into my mom's lap, all of them at the same time. They hung out at our house and became my friends. Our home became a place where kids could come and be. My mother hugged them, she listened to them, she loved them. For a lot of those kids, it was the only little bit of light and love they had in their lives.

Anything my mother ever had, she shared, not just with family or friends but with anybody. If her tomato plants produced more than two tomatoes, she'd be bringing those tomatoes to church or setting out a basket in the front yard with a sign that said "Free Tomatoes." Because of how generous my mom was, I had no idea how poor we really were when I was a child. She has spent her life caring for others, sharing resources, raising money for others, giving up her time.

That is an actual philanthropist right there.

And because of her, I decided to pursue a career in healing work. I came very, very close to being a minister. I got my master's in health care administration at the University of North Carolina at Chapel Hill, and then, at 28, I took my first job at a foundation, where each year I gave away $25 million to $30 million to support health care in low-income communities. For a while, I felt like the luckiest man on the planet, coming from where I had, earning handsomely for doing what I thought was sacred work of love.

As I started off on the journey, I felt about my work in philanthropy what adrienne maree brown, a facilitator and futurist, writes in her beautiful book *Emergent Strategy*:

> When we are engaged in acts of love, we humans are at our best and most resilient. The love in romance that makes us want to be better people, the love of children that makes us change our whole lives to meet their needs, the love of family that makes us drop everything to take care of them, the love of community that makes us work tirelessly with broken hearts. Perhaps humans' core function is love.[1]

Sixteen years in the field have shown me that actual philanthropists—those like my mother, engaged in acts of love for humanity—are much more prevalent among the regular population and are only rarely found inside the field's formal institutions, the foundations. Honestly, the vast majority of foundations have no right to call what they do "philanthropy." The word isn't "egoanthropy," "expertanthropy," or "ROI-anthropy." But in the field, instead of love of humanity, there is a lot of the opposite: ego, greed, fear, blame, and disrespect.

～～～

"That word philanthropy has been so abused," says Donna, my philanthropy mentor and fellow Lumbee Indian.

> Organized philanthropy has done a disservice to philanthropy. When people see the word "philanthropy," they automatically think of dollars. In the organized field of philanthropy, philanthropy is something we "do." For me, it's not that. I'm not

doing philanthropy; I'm *being* it. There's a difference between acting as a philanthropist and being a philanthropist. When you're *being* something, it infuses who you are and your contemplation into it. You connect with the things that resonate with your being, and your life is a testament to that. That was the way I was raised, *to be, rather than to seem*, which is the state motto of North Carolina.[2]

Donna has been my "philanthropy mother" since I got started in the field. She got involved in philanthropy a couple decades earlier than I did, and she happens to come from the very same land as my people come from, Robeson County, North Carolina. Like most Natives, and especially the elders, her answers to theoretical questions are rooted in home and family—literally Indigenous:

> My father, bless his heart, he would be one hundred and twelve now if he was alive. He passed when he was seventy. His way of leadership was quiet and powerful. I didn't know everything he had been involved with until he died. People at the funeral coming up to me saying, "If it wasn't for your father, I wouldn't have a job," you know, Indian teachers and others. That's the philanthropy that I grew up with; that was the giving. We were of course poor as church mice. When he died, it was just a little over three thousand dollars a year that was coming into the house, and he raised ten children on that. As poor as anyone was, we didn't go to bed hungry; we were taken care of. He was disabled from the time I was in second grade, from cancer. He lived decades longer than they predicted he would. At the times when he was sickest, we had the most

food we ever had, because that was the traditional way of the community. There was an infrastructure of giving.

Daddy was my mentor in politics. It wasn't about getting credit; it wasn't about what you did; it was what the outcome was, if it helped somebody. I grew up watching all the local politicians come to our house, and it was a house that didn't have indoor plumbing, still had the front porch kind of wood shack kind of thing. But it was built on love and it lasted . . . it's still standing after sixty-five-some years. It was the highly segregated part of the county, and yet people of all colors and stripes would come into our house all the time. That's what he believed in, they believed in, Mama and Daddy.

He would sit in front of the gas station with his buddy. People would come by and talk to him and he would give his opinion of the election and so forth. Politicians visited because they knew he could turn the election to their favor, sitting out in front of that gas station. I called him "the mayor" after I saw the movie *Do the Right Thing*, because the mayor was the one who sat on the front step and did that. That was Daddy; that's what he did. So that's the cultural context I'm rooted in, when I came to philanthropy.

My own grandfather was the same way. He lived in Hope Mills, North Carolina, at the end of a dirt road that you couldn't even get to if it was raining. When he passed away, there were hundreds of people who came to his funeral, whose lives he had touched and I'd had no idea. I knew he spent a few days each week visiting men in the county jail. I had never known he had become the chaplain for Cumberland County in an official capacity. At his funeral, one after another, people stood and said, "I was in jail, your granddaddy talked to me and changed my life, and now I'm doing this, this, and this." I had no idea, because he was just my quiet, very quiet, simple grandfather.

Donna nods, hearing about my grandfather. "We are the original philanthropists, Natives," she says. "I mean Indigenous people worldwide. It's so obvious that this is an Indigenous way. It's not a Lumbee way, Navajo way, or a Maori way. It's an Indigenous way that cuts across continents, the original way of being and giving."

This was echoed in my interview with Dana Arviso, the former executive director of the Potlatch Fund. She told me the story of a conversation she'd led about poverty reduction strategies among a gathering of Natives in the Cheyenne River territory. "They told me they don't have a word for poverty," she said. "The closest thing that they had as an explanation for poverty was 'to be without family.'" Which is basically unheard of. "They were saying it was a foreign concept to them that someone could be just so isolated and without any sort of a safety net or a family or a sense of kinship that they would be suffering from poverty," she continued. Dana is Navajo, and we compared notes on the traditions in our respective communities.

"If someone is sick or if someone passes away, you will never lack for food," I told her. "It's just like the food comes out the woodwork. If you're sick, there's a system in place to make sure that food and support are coming your way."

"Absolutely," she agreed.

There's a lot of showing up with food, showing up to help and sit with people in time of mourning.

Just showing up. I mean, that's one of the biggest lessons I learned from my family: you may not know what to do, but you better show up. Whether that means sharing food, sharing firewood, sharing whatever you had. Taking in extended family because they're going through a rough time and raising their kids. I think that's the biggest difference I see between kind of this mainstream framework and Native communities is that there's such a focus on individualism. And in our communities it's like, no, we are not a healthy community if we're not taking care of everybody.[3]

We are not a healthy community unless we're taking care of everybody, and I mean all our relations, inside and outside our tribes.

~~~~

Philanthropy and charitable acts are often called altruistic. Altruism is about doing things for others, unselfishly, without expectation of reward or acknowledgment, and maybe even at some cost to oneself. In zoology, altruism is a little more extreme. It's usually an action that benefits the rest of the species at the actual expense of the individual, like an ant who allows her sisters and brothers to use her body as a bridge across water and then drowns. In human behavior, it's meant less literally—there's no expectation that a donor is dying for the cause. Still, there's an aspect of self-sacrifice. Many people hold this kind of self-sacrifice for others as the highest form of generosity and kindness.

In 2020, MacKenzie Scott, an author and ex-wife of Amazon founder Jeff Bezos, to whom she was married for 25 years, donated close to $6 billion. To donate so much, so quickly, when everything in our society supports the hoarding of wealth, is countercultural. There is no question her gifts will do good for the people who receive those funds—particularly those supporting antiracism work and organizations led by people of color. Yet that cannot be the end of the story. We cannot applaud the gift without considering how it was made possible and why it was needed in the first place. When we hear of massive donations from the super-rich, we should consider it less a sign of goodwill and more an indication of a system that is far out of whack. Scott even noted the real impacts of historical and systemic racism on the wealth gap in her first giving announcement: "There's no question in my mind that anyone's personal wealth is the product of a collective effort, and of social structures which present opportunities to some people, and obstacles to countless others."

Yet . . . how often is it called altruism when sacrifices are made by people from whom we assume and expect selflessness? We don't call it altruism when a mother stays awake all night by her child's bedside. We don't even call it altruism when a home care worker stays way beyond overtime, until the hurricane has blown over, to ensure the safety of her elderly charge. We *expect* certain kinds of people to make sacrifices. Apparently, we reserve the term "altruism" for the privileged, fortunate, entitled people for whom self-sacrifice is a stretch, is unexpected.

The anthropologist David Graeber notes that small societies without money or markets (like Indigenous tribes in the Amazon basin or in Papua New Guinea) don't even possess words in their vocabularies for either "altruism" or "self-interest." Those two extremes oversimplify the reason for human interactions around giving, sharing, and hoarding resources, he says, which are always reflective of much more complicated motivations, including solidarity, pride, desire, envy, the anticipation of shared enjoyment, and so on. It's the entire web of our relationships that are at the core of our generosity.[4]

When you look more closely, altruism is actually a fundamental reflection of the separation paradigm, the Us versus Them mindset. Linguistically, it's literally about Other-ing—the word comes from the Latin root *alter*, "other." Altruism also is a linear concept; it moves in one direction, from the Have to the Have-Not, a one-way flow of resources. Altruism is the poster child for white saviors.

The Native worldview shifts the focus from altruism to reciprocity. Reciprocity is based on our fundamental interconnection—there is no Other, no Us versus Them, no Haves versus Have-Nots. Reciprocity is the sense that I'm going to give to you because I know you would do the same for me. No one is just a giver or just a taker; we're all each at some point in our lives. This also reflects a cyclical dynamic, as opposed to a one-off, one-way relationship. The Native botanist Robin Wall Kimmerer writes in her book *Braiding Sweetgrass*, "Reciprocity is a matter of keeping the gift in motion through self-perpetuating cycles of giving and receiving. . . . Through reciprocity the gift is replenished. All of our flourishing is mutual."[5]

The Native principle of reciprocity is where the white colonizers and settlers got the concept of "Indian giver." Natives expressed that any gift was given within the expectation of an ongoing relationship, the idea that I give you this because I know you would (and will, at some point) do the same for me. Mutual dependence is necessary for social well-being. We are symbiotic. All of our flourishing is mutual. The white people got all holier-than-thou about it, claiming that a gift isn't actually a gift unless there's no expectation of return. But the cyclical nature of reciprocity is actually the truth of things. As the cultural scholar Lewis Hyde describes in his book *The Gift*, the very essence of a gift, as contrasted with a commodity, is its *relational* quality. Gifts aren't actually "free," even when they don't cost anything. There are always strings attached; a gift is always tied to a relationship.

One of the most moving gestures during the height of the COVID-19 pandemic in 2020 was when the people of Ireland raised millions of dollars to send to the Navajo and Hopi Nations, who were hit especially hard by the virus. It turns out that in 1847, during the Potato Famine that devastated Ireland, the Chocktaw Nation, which didn't have much to spare, managed to collect $170 (the equivalent of more than $5,000 today) to send to starving families in Ireland. The act of kindness was never forgotten, and it forged a solidarity between the nations. In 2020, things came full circle as hundreds of Irish people donated more than $2 million, nearly 200 years later. This is reciprocity!

The lesson here is that the supposed selflessness of pure altruism doesn't exist. There's really no such thing as the self completely disconnected from what's outside the self, the Other. What's truer to the way things really are—interconnected and interdependent—is reciprocity. Reciprocity means we are only a healthy community if we're taking care of everybody.

～～～

In 2016, Natives received a lot of positive media coverage and solidarity around the Standing Rock protests. In the spring of 2016, a call went out on the Standing Rock Sioux Indian Reservation to stop the proposed 1,172-mile Dakota

Access Pipeline. Standing Rock sits on the border of North Dakota and South Dakota, and the pipeline threatens not only the reservation's vital water source, sacred lands, and ancestral burial grounds but also the aquifer of the Missouri River, which provides drinking water to 10 million Americans.[6] The call was answered—and echoed—by thousands of people across the United States and beyond, from both Native and orphan peoples.

Standing Rock was a historic moment, a gathering of tribes that hadn't been seen in more than 100 years. I want to underscore this. Native Americans are not one lump of homogenous people. We differ starkly in our ways, and we're often at odds with one another. We sometimes compete for federal support or fishing rights. In the end, though, we're soaking in the same colonized atmosphere as the rest of the country (and globe), and we're infected by the colonizer virus and internalized oppression just as other communities are. So the fact that all the tribes put aside their differences and came together to support the Sioux over the contested black snake of a pipeline was a big deal.

Standing Rock—a camp of 4,000 to 5,000 people strong at its height—was managed by a distributed leadership structure involving elders, women, and youth, using community assembly meetings and technology to organize. Photographer Camille Seaman of the Shinnecock Nation reflected on her time at the encampment:

> Before dawn every day, a rider on horseback (or, sometimes, a driver in a car) would make their way through camp, saying, "Good morning, my relatives! It's a beautiful day. Wake up, and remember why you are here!" Then we would all

gather in a circle and pray as the sun rose. Our prayers would be for those who opposed us, those who supported us from afar, and those who were among us. These prayers continued all day and all night in many forms. In the evening, the sounds of singing and of drums (our mother's heartbeat) could be heard in the dark.[7]

Prayer, ritual, ceremony were everywhere and constant. "The whole time, you are in ceremony," said activist AnaYelsi Velasco-Sanchez, who volunteered in the kitchens. "You wake in a space committed to prayer, every action is referred to as an act of prayer. If you are working in the kitchen and you are preparing this food, you are preparing medicine for the people. Prayer was embodied in the space; it was a posture you took."[8]

Predictably, heart-wrenchingly, the militarized police force turned out to protect the interests of the oil business. One observer, who volunteered as a medic, witnessed the police:

> ripping elders in the midst of prayer out of sweat lodge, forcing hundreds of people peacefully assembled to strip and stand naked, spraying hundreds of people peacefully assembled with water and chemical weapons in freezing cold weather, barricading the access to advanced health care response, blockading the arrival of supplies to keep people healthy and warm in the winter, and shooting sponge grenades and explosive devices at people's faces, groins, and limbs, causing blindness and ripped open flesh.[9]

It was a moment in which the dynamics of today's world surfaced starkly and undeniably: the tension between the interconnected, reverential Native worldview on the one hand and the violent, exploitative ways of the colonizer on the other.

～～～

If my heart cracked when the camp was broken down, it shattered at the results of the 2016 presidential election and the ensuing four years of emboldened racism and terrorization of immigrant communities that unfolded during the Trump presidency. I told Donna, my philanthropy mother, how I just wanted to retreat and avoid white people after that. She told me that it was a symptom of colonization that I felt that way. And she shared this story:

> Years back, around 1992, I was at the youth and elders gathering at Onondaga. I was in the cookhouse, the community space—we did everything there, shower and hang out and meet, as well as, yes, cook and eat, so it was called the cookhouse. It was the end of the gathering, so we were getting ready to leave. We were packing up, and there was an elder sitting at the table with the youth. That's the way learning was done.
>
> I was ready to leave. But then I heard him say, "Europeans coming to this land was not a problem."
>
> As an elder, he had memories of some of the historic activities of [atrocities by] the U.S. government against Native people. So when I heard him say that, I decided I had to stay and listen to him.
>
> "The problem was," he went on, "they forgot their teachings."

I'll never forget that moment. Because it just opened my heart. There are people who remember the teachings, non-Indigenous too. But Indigenous peoples are a living reminder. We're not gone, no matter how many times they tried to make us invisible. We're here as a living reminder. That's what we can be to all institutions, if we're allowed to be.[10]

As Desmond Tutu writes in *The Book of Forgiving*: "When we assault another's humanity, we assault our own humanity. Every person wants to be acknowledged and affirmed for who and what they are, a human being of infinite worth, someone with a place in the world. We can't violate another's dignity without violating our own. Violence, whether in words or deeds, only begets more violence."[11]

It made me remember footage I'd seen of a young woman at Standing Rock. The day after she and her fellow Water Protectors had been assaulted by the militarized police and National Guard using fire hoses and Mace and rubber bullets—the very next day—she trudged back to the armed forces with candy in her hands. The Water Protector walked right back up to the same guards and police, moving slowly, her open palms offering the sweets, the way you might approach a feral animal, and she said, "It's not you. We know it's not your fault. We're not mad at you; we're praying for you." That young woman was reminding them of a different way to be. *Mitakuye Oyasin*—all my relations. We are all related, all connected. The Native way is to bring the oppressor into our circle of healing. Healing cannot occur unless everyone is part of the process. Let it begin.

Notes

Introduction: What if Money Could Heal Us

1. Because this book focuses on race-based disparities, there will not be much if any mention of gender and the wealth of women compared to men. But the dynamics are similar in many ways. The gender wealth gap is far greater than the often-mentioned wage gap (i.e., that women earn 77 to 80 cents for every dollar a man earns on average). Single white women have just 32 cents for every dollar of wealth that single men do. The disparity is much greater for single women of color, who have "only pennies on the dollar compared to white men," according to Diana Farrell and Karen Persichilli Keogh, "The Gender Wage Gap Gets a Lot of Attention, but Another Metric Is Even More Disconcerting," *Business Insider*, May 15, 2017, http://www.businessinsider.de/jpmorgan-on-gender-wealth-gap-2017-5.

   The top 25 richest people in the U.S. on the 2016 *Forbes* 400 had a combined net worth of over $900 billion and are all white. Of them, Alice Walton (13th place), Jacqueline Mars (16th place, sharing it with her husband, John Mars—yes, like the candy), and Laurene Powell Jobs (23rd place) are the only women. Of the next 25 places, 23 are occupied by white men, the remaining two by white women. Chase Peterson-Withorn, "Forbes 400: The Full List of the Richest People in America 2016," *Forbes*, October 4, 2016, https://www.forbes.com/sites/chasewithorn/2016/10/04/forbes-400-the-full-list-of-the-richest-people-in-america-2016.

   As for the people working in financial services (banking, insurance, asset management, and professional services firms like Deloitte and PricewaterhouseCoopers), only one in four of those who reach a senior role is female, according to a 2017 study by the *Financial Times*. Laura Noonan, Alan Smith, David Blood, and Martin Stabe, "Women Still Miss Out on Management in Finance," *Financial Times*, April 4, 2017, https://ig.ft.com/managements-missing-women-data.

2. Ken Stern, "Why the Rich Don't Give to Charity," *The Atlantic*, April 2013, https://www.theatlantic.com/magazine/archive/2013/04/why-the-rich-dont-give/309254.

3. Council on Foundations, "2020 Grantmaker Salary and Benefits Report: Key Findings," https://www.cof.org/content/2020-grantmaker-salary-and-benefits-report-key-findings.

4. H. Art Taylor, "It's Time for Greater Foundation Board Diversity," *Forbes*, September 18, 2020, https://www.forbes.com/sites/forbesnonprofitcouncil/2020/09/18/its-time-for-greater-foundation-board-diversity/?sh=72c0c4e21af1.

5. Julia Travers, "The Hardest Hit: Who Is Supporting Communities of Color During COVID-19?," *Inside Philanthropy*, April 4, 2020, https://www.insidephilanthropy.com/home/2020/4/2/the-hardest-hit-who-is-supporting-communities-of-color-during-covid-19, based on research in Philanthropic Initiative for Racial Equity, "What Does Philanthropy Need to Ask to Deepen Investments for Racial and Gender Justice?," https://racialequity.org/wp-content/uploads/2019/11/1126_PRE_Infographic_final.pdf.

6. McKinsey & Company, "Racial Equity in Financial Services," September 10, 2020, https://www.mckinsey.com/industries/financial-services/our-insights/racial-equity-in-financial-services#.

7. Megan Rose Dickey, "Venture Capital's Diversity Disaster," *Techcrunch*, July 30, 2018, https://techcrunch.com/2018/07/30/venture-capitals-diversity-disaster.

8. Taylor Soper, "Who Are U.S. Angel Investors? Study Shows 78% Male; 87% White; 17% in California," *GeekWire*, November 28, 2017, https://www.geekwire.com/2017/u-s-angel-investors-study-shows-78-male-87-white-17-california.

9. "This difference persists even after accounting for credit scores and net worth of founders." Victor Hwang, Sameeksha Desai, and Ross Baird, *Access to Capital for Entrepreneurs: Removing Barriers*, Ewing Marion Kauffman Foundation, 2019, https://www.kauffman.org/wp-content/uploads/2020/06/Access-To-Capital_2019.pdf.

10. Galen Gruman, "Minority Tech Startups in the U.S. Have Seen Almost No Progress in VC Funding," *Computerworld*, October 7, 2020, https://www.computerworld.com/article/3584734/minority-tech-startups-in-the-us-have-seen-almost-no-progress-in-vc-funding.html, based on data from *Crunchbase Diversity Spotlight 2020: Funding to Black & Latinx Founders*, Crunchbase, http://about.crunchbase.com/wp-content/uploads/2020/10/2020_crunchbase_diversity_report.pdf.

11. Malcolm X, "The Harlem 'Hate-Gang' Scare," in *Malcolm X Speaks* (New York: Pathfinder, 1989), 68–69. He said this in response to a question during the question period following his speech at the Militant Labor Forum, held in New York on May 29, 1964.

12. David Graeber, *Debt: The First 5,000 Years* (New York: Melville House, 2011), 47.

Part One: Where It Hurts

1. Audre Lorde, "The Master's Tools Will Never Dismantle the Master's House," *Sister Outsider* (Berkeley, CA: Ten Speed Press, 1984), 110–113.

Chapter One: Stolen and Sold

1. Renee Danielle Singh, "Our Roots Go Back to Roanoke: Investigating the Link between the Lost Colony and the Lumbee People of North Carolina," student paper, University of California, Davis, 2006. Also see Malinda Maynor Lowery, *Lumbee Indians in the Jim Crow South* (Chapel Hill: University of North Carolina Press, 2010).

2. Brian Murphy, "Wait Continues for Lumbee Tribe. Federal Recognition Not Included in Congressional Deal," *News & Observer*, December 21, 2020, https://www.newsobserver.com/news/politics-government/article248002425.html.

3. Priscilla Long, "Duwamish Tribe Wins Federal Recognition on January 19, 2001, but Loses It Again Two Days Later," HistoryLink.org, January 20, 2001, http://www.historylink.org/File/2951.

4. Shall I recommend some? *An Indigenous Peoples' History of the United States*, by Roxanne Dunbar-Ortiz. *The Origin of Others*, by Toni Morrison. *Racecraft: The Soul of Equality in American Life*, by Barbara E. Fields and Karen J. Fields. *Sacred Economics: Money, Gift, and Society in the Age of Transition*, by Charles Eisenstein.

5. Derek Rasmussen, "Stemming the Tide of De-Indigenization," plenary talk at the Economics of Happiness conference, Portland, Oregon, February 2015. https://www.youtube.com/watch?v=cr87shQNnYA.

6. Robin DiAngelo, "No, I Won't Stop Saying 'White Supremacy,'" *YES!*, June 30, 2017, http://www.yesmagazine.org/people-power/no-i-wont-stop-saying -white-supremacy-20170630.

7. Vanessa Daniel, "America Is Burning," *Medium*, September 13, 2017, https:// medium.com/@GroundswellFund/americaisburning-4f154e201a3a.

8. DiAngelo, "No, I Won't Stop Saying 'White Supremacy.'"

9. Jon Stone, "British People Are Proud of Colonialism and the British Empire, Poll Finds," *The Independent*, January 19, 2016, http://www.independent. co.uk/news/uk/politics/british-people-are-proud-of-colonialism-and-the -british-empire-poll-finds-a6821206.html.

10. Will Dahlgreen, "The British Empire Is 'Something to Be Proud Of,'" YouGov, July 26, 2014, https://yougov.co.uk/news/2014/07/26/ britain-proud-its-empire/.

11. Albert Memmi, *The Colonizer and the Colonized* (New York: Viking Adult, 1965), 64. Emphasis added.

12. National Congress of American Indians, "Indian Country Demographics," http://www.ncai.org/about-tribes/demographics, citing 2010 U.S. Census.

13. The median household income of Native households in 2015 was $38,530, compared with $55,775 across the nation as a whole. Data from the 2015 American Community Survey, cited by Levi Rickert, "U.S. Census Bureau: Native American Statistics," *Native News Online*, November 24, 2016, https:// nativenewsonline.net/currents/u-s-census-bureau-native-american-statistics/.

14. The dropout rate for Natives is 30 percent (47 percent for those in Bureau of Indian Education schools), compared to the national dropout average of 18 percent. A more jarring statistic: while more than 60 percent of average high school students go on to college, only 17 percent of Natives continue to college. Helen Oliff, "Graduation Rates and American Indian Education," Partnership with Native Americans, May 16, 2017, http://blog .nativepartnership.org/graduation-rates-american-indian-education.

15. Centers for Disease Control and Prevention's National Center for Health Statistics, National Vital Statistics System Mortality Data 2012–2013. Database available at http://wonder.cdc.gov/ucd-icd10.html.

16. Emily Erasim and Osprey Orielle Lake, "Women on the Front Lines Fighting Fracking in the Bakken Oil Shale Formations, "*EcoWatch*, March 12, 2016, http://ecowatch.com/2016/03/12/women-frontlines-fighting-fracking, citing U.S. Department of Justice records.

17. Kenrya Rankin, "Report: Juvenile Justice System Is Failing Native Youth," *Colorlines*, August 3, 2015, http://www.colorlines.com/articles/report-juvenile-justice -system-failing-native-youth.

18. Based on data from the Centers for Disease Control and Prevention. See Chelsea Cirruzzo, "Study: COVID-19 Mortality Twice as High Among Native Americans," *U.S. News & World Report*, December 10, 2020, https://www.usnews.com/news/health-news/articles/2020-12-10/ covid-mortality-twice-as-high-among-native-americans-than-whites.

19. Sahir Doshi, Allison Jordan, Kate Kelly, and Danyelle Solomon, "The COVID-19 Response in Indian Country: A Federal Failure," Center for American Progress, June 18, 2020, https://americanprogress.org/issues/green/ reports/2020/06/18/486480/covid-19-response-indian-country.

20. Indian Health Service, "Disparities," Fact sheet, https://www.ihs.gov/ newsroom/factsheets/disparities (accessed April 2018).

21. Urban Indian Health Institute, "Health Disparities in UIHO Service Areas," Fact sheet, http://www.uihi.org/wp-content/uploads/2017/08/UIHO_Fact -Sheet_20150227.pdf (accessed February 2021).

22. Dan Hurley, "Grandma's Experiences Leave Mark on Your Genes," *Discover*, May 2013, http://discovermagazine.com/2013/may/13-grandmas -experiences-leave-epigenetic-mark-on-your-genes.

23. Frantz Fanon, *The Wretched of the Earth* (New York: Grove Press, 1964), 36.

24. Adom Getachew, "Colonialism Made the Modern World. Let's Remake It." *New York Times*, July 27, 2020, https://www.nytimes.com/2020/07/27/opinion/ sunday/decolonization-statues.html.

25. Delilah Friedler, "Indigenous Land Acknowledgement, Explained," *Teen Vogue*, February 8, 2018, https://www.teenvogue.com/story/indigenous-land -acknowledgement-explained.

Chapter Two: Arriving at the Plantation

1. Reynolds history is from author's experiences, supplemented with information from Patrick Reynolds and Tom Schachtman, *The Gilded Leaf: Triumph, Tragedy, and Tobacco: Three Generations of the R.J. Reynolds Family and Fortune* (Boston: Little, Brown, 1989).

2. Anonymous, interview by author, July 18, 2017.

3. Anonymous, interview by author, July 23, 2017.

4. Jess Rimington and Joanna Levitt Cea, "Decolonizing Design," September 2016, draft shared with the author, from the forthcoming book *The Recollective Way*.

5. Kenneth Jones and Tema Okun, "White Supremacy Culture," from *Dismantling Racism: A Workbook for Social Change Groups* (ChangeWork, 2001), http://www.cwsworkshop.org/PARC_site_B/dr-culture.html.

Chapter Three: House Slaves

1. Anonymous, interview by author, July 10, 2017.

2. Anonymous, interview by author, April 10, 2017.

3. Anonymous, interview by author, April 10, 2017.

4. Anonymous, interview by author, July 18, 2017.

5. Anonymous, interview by author, April 10, 2017.

6. Anonymous, interview by author, April 12, 2017.

7. Anonymous, interview by author, July 26, 2017.

8. Anonymous, interview by author, July 20, 2017.

9. Anonymous, interview by author, July 18, 2017.

10. Gerri Spilka, Vivian Figueredo, and Georgia Kioukis, *Foundations Facilitate Diversity, Equity, and Inclusion: Partnering with Community and Nonprofits*, OMG Center for Collaborative Learning, http://www.d5coalition.org/wp-content/uploads/2014/08/D5_OMGreport_072814-1.pdf, p. 8.

11. Anonymous, interview by author, April 12, 2017.

12. LM Strategies on behalf of ABFE, *The Exit Interview: Perceptions on Why Black Professionals Leave Grantmaking Institutions*, May 2014, http://www.abfe.org/wp-content/uploads/2014/05/ABFE-The-Exit-Interview.pdf.

13. Anonymous, interview by author, July 20, 2017.

14. Council on Foundations, *2020 Grantmaker Salary and Benefits Report: Key Findings*, https://www.cof.org/content/2020-grantmaker-salary-and-benefits-report-key-findings.

15. Gara LaMarche, "Democracy and the Donor Class," *Democracy* 34 (Fall 2014), https://democracyjournal.org/magazine/34/democracy-and-the-donor-class.

16. McKinsey & Company, "Racial Equity in Financial Services," September 10, 2020, https://www.mckinsey.com/industries/financial-services/our-insights/racial-equity-in-financial-services#.

17. Megan Rose Dickey, "Venture Capital's Diversity Disaster," *Techcrunch*, July 30, 2018, https://techcrunch.com/2018/07/30/venture-capitals-diversity-disaster, citing data from Richard Kerby, "Where Did You Go to School?," *Noteworthy*, July 30, 2018, https://blog.usejournal.com/where-did-you-go-to-school-bde54d846188.

18. Taylor Soper, "Who Are U.S. Angel Investors? Study Shows 78% male; 87% white; 17% in California," *GeekWire*, November 28, 2017, https://www.geekwire.com/2017/u-s-angel-investors-study-shows-78-male-87-white-17-california.

19. Michael A. Cohen, Maria Figueroa Küpçü, and Parag Khanna, "The New Colonialists," *Foreign Policy* (November–December 2008), reprinted online in *Utne Reader*, http://www.utne.com/politics/the-new-colonialists.

20. Patrick Caldwell, "The Financial Industry Doesn't Want You to Know about Its Lack of Diversity," *Mother Jones*, March 11, 2014, https://www.motherjones.com/politics/2014/03/financial-firm-diversity-jobs.

21. Vu Le, "Are You Guilty of Fakequity? If So, What to Do About It," *Nonprofit AF*, http://nonprofitaf.com/2015/03/are-you-guilty-of-fakequity-if-so-what-to-do-about-it.

22. Anonymous, interview by author, July 26, 2017.

23. Anonymous, interview by author, August 14, 2017.

24. Anonymous, interview by author, July 10, 2017.

25. Floyd Mills, *The State of Change: An Analysis of Women and People of Color in the Philanthropic Sector*, Council on Foundations, July 27, 2017, https://www .cof.org/sites/default/files/documents/files/2017-Gender-Diversity-Report .pdf. See also Mark Hrywna, "Little Progress on Staff, Executive Diversity," *NonProfit Times*, July 28, 2017, http://www.thenonprofittimes.com/ news-articles/little-progress-diversity-staff.

26. Frank Dobbin and Alexandra Kalev, "Why Diversity Programs Fail," *Harvard Business Review* (July–August 2016), https://hbr.org/2016/07/ why-diversity-programs-fail.

27. Andrea Armeni, interview by author, December 18, 2017.

28. Chris Cardona, interview by author, June 15, 2017.

29. Ryan Bowers, interview by author, December 10, 2017.

Chapter Four: Field Hands

1. Chris Cardona, interview by author, June 15, 2017.

2. Anonymous, interview by author, July 1, 2017.

3. adrienne maree brown, *Emergent Strategy: Shaping Change, Changing Worlds* (Oakland: AK Press, 2017).

4. Vu Le, "In the Trump Era, Nonprofits Need a New Social Contract with Foundations," Philanthropy.com, November 14, 2016, https://www .philanthropy.com/article/Opinion-In-the-Trump-Era/238408.

5. Anonymous, interview by author, July 15, 2017.

6. Will Pittz and Rinku Sen, *Short Changed: Foundation Giving and Communities of Color*, Applied Research Center, Spring 2004, https://drive.google.com/ file/d/1KdG8vQtwAno0jGySRD8XdfOHBud5wj6b/view.

7. Rick Cohen, "Data Snapshot on Racial Justice Grantmaking," *Critical Issues Forum: Moving Forward on Racial Justice Philanthropy* 5 (June 2014): 38–42, http://racialequity.org/docs/CIF5.pdf.

8. Julia Travers "The Hardest Hit: Who Is Supporting Communities of Color During COVID-19?," *Inside Philanthropy*, April 4, 2020, https://www .insidephilanthropy.com/home/2020/4/2/the-hardest-hit-who-is-supporting -communities-of-color-during-covid-19, based on research in Philanthropic Initiative for Racial Equity, "What Does Philanthropy Need to Ask to Deepen Investments for Racial and Gender Justice?," https://racialequity.org/ wp-content/uploads/2019/11/1126_PRE_Infographic_final.pdf.

9. Robert Fairlie, Alicia Robb, and David T. Robinson, "Black and White: Access to Capital among Minority-Owned Startups" (Stanford, CA: Stanford Institute for Economic Policy Research, 2016), https://siepr.stanford.edu/sites/default/ files/publications/17-003.pdf.

10. Note from Jessica Norwood, November 13, 2016. See also http://www .therunwayproject.org.

11. Galen Gruman, "Minority Tech Startups in the U.S. Have Seen Almost No Progress in VC Funding," *Computerworld*, October 7, 2020, https://www.computerworld.com/article/3584734/minority-tech-startups-in-the-us-have-seen-almost-no-progress-in-vc-funding.html, based on data from *Crunchbase Diversity Spotlight 2020: Funding to Black & Latinx Founders*, Crunchbase, http://about.crunchbase.com/wp-content/uploads/2020/10/2020_crunchbase_diversity_report.pdf.

12. Anonymous, interview by author, December 10, 2017.

13. Debbie Gruentstein Bocian, Wei Li, and Keith Ernst, "Foreclosures by Race and Ethnicity: The Demographics of a Crisis," Center for Responsible Lending, June 18, 2010, http://www.responsiblelending.org/mortgage-lending/research-analysis/foreclosures-by-race-and-ethnicity.pdf.

14. Ryan Bowers, interview by author, December 12, 2017.

Chapter Five: The Overseers

1. Terrance Keenan, *The Promise at Hand: Prospects for Foundation Leadership in the 1990s* (Robert Wood Johnson Foundation, 1992). Available at http://www.policyarchive.org/handle/10207/21820.

2. Terrance Keenan obituary, *New York Times*, March 7, 2009, https://archive.nytimes.com/query.nytimes.com/gst/fullpage-9F0DE7D7153AF934A35750C0A96F9C8B63.html.

3. Paul Lukas, with Maggie Overfelt, "UPS United Parcel Service: James Casey Transformed a Tiny Messenger Service into the World's Largest Shipper by Getting All Wrapped Up in the Details of Package Delivery," CNN Money, April 1, 2003, http://money.cnn.com/magazines/fsb/fsb_archive/2003/04/01/341024.

4. Martin Luther King Jr., "Where Do We Go from Here?," speech delivered at the Southern Christian Leadership Conference, Atlanta, GA, August 16, 1967.

Chapter Six: Freedom

1. adrienne maree brown, *Emergent Strategy* (Oakland: AK Press, 2017).

2. Donna Chavis, interview by author, August 17, 2017.

3. Quoted in Jenara Nerenberg, "Why Are So Many Adults Today Haunted by Trauma?," *Greater Good Magazine*, June 8, 2017, https://greatergood.berkeley.edu/article/item/why_are_so_many_adults_today_haunted_by_trauma.

Chapter Seven: Medicine Beyond Money

1. Alex Daniels, "Companies Lead Philanthropic Response to Calls for Racial Justice," *Chronicle of Philanthropy*, August 24, 2020, https://www.philanthropy.com/article/companies-lead-philanthropic-response-to-calls-for-racial-justice-but-will-it-last?cid=gen_sign_in.

2. Carlie Porterfield, "France Would Return African Artifacts through Proposed New Law," *Forbes*, July 16, 2020, https://www.forbes.com/sites/carlieporterfield/2020/07/16/france-would-return-african-artifacts-through-proposed-new-law/?sh=305bee054e0d.

3. Killian Fox, "Are Ghosts Haunting the British Museum?," *The Economist*, April 28, 2020, https://www.economist.com/1843/2020/04/28/are-ghosts-haunting-the-british-museum.

4. Rob Hopkins, "What If Imagination Were a Universal Human Right?," interview with Masum Momaya and Ariane Conrad, *From What If to What Next*, episode 6, podcast audio, August 3, 2020, https://www.robhopkins.net/2020/08/03/from-what-if-to-what-next-episode-six.

5. Richard Kwame Krah, "Meet the Activist Who Boldly Reclaims Artifacts Stolen from Africa during Slavery," *Eyegambia*, November 22, 2020, https://eyegambia.org/meet-the-activist-who-boldly-reclaims-artifacts-stolen-from-africa-during-slavery.

6. Fox, "Are Ghosts Haunting the British Museum?"

7. The story of the museum's poor choice is covered in Brian Boucher, "A Museum Canceled a Show about Police Brutality. Here's the Art," *New York Times*, June 9, 2020, https://www.nytimes.com/2020/06/09/arts/design/moca-cleveland-shaun-leonardo.html.

8. Eve Tuck and K. Wayne Yang, "Decolonization Is Not a Metaphor," *Decolonization: Indigeneity, Education & Society* 1, no. 1, 2012: 1–40, https://clas.osu.edu/sites/clas.osu.edu/files/Tuck%20and%20Yang%202012%20Decolonization%20is%20not%20a%20metaphor.pdf.

9. "NDN Collective LANDBACK Campaign Launching on Indigenous Peoples' Day 2020," NDN Collective, October 9, 2020, https://ndncollective.org/ndn-collective-landback-campaign-launching-on-indigenous-peoples-day-2020.

Chapter Eight: Story as Medicine

1. Atlas of the Future, https://atlasofthefuture.org/project/human-library.

2. Bridgit Antoinette Evans (bridgitaevans), "I am Bridgit Antoinette Evans from the Pop Culture Collaborative . . . ," Reddit, https://www.reddit.com/r/IAmA/comments/8ha5uq/i_am_bridgit_antoinette_evans_from_the_pop.

3. Marshall Ganz, "Telling Your Public Story: Self, Us, Now," Kennedy School of Government, 2007, https://www.welcomingrefugees.org/sites/default/files/documents/resources/Public%20Story%20Worksheet07Ganz.pdf.

Part Three: How to Heal

1. Peter Block, *Community: The Structure of Belonging* (Oakland, CA: Berrett-Koehler, 2008).

Step One: Grieve

1. Stephen Jenkinson, "Orphan Wisdom," https://orphanwisdom.com/about. Please don't miss his important, gorgeous book *Die Wise* (Berkeley, CA: North Atlantic Books, 2015).

2. Aurora Levins Morales, *Medicine Stories* (Boston: South End Press, 1999).

3. Hilary Giovale, interview by author, August 20, 2017.

4. Peter Buffett, interview by author, December 10, 2017.

5. Mias deKlerk. "Healing Emotional Trauma in Organizations: An O.D. Framework and Case Study," *Organization Development Journal* 25 (Summer 2007).

6. Bourree Lam, "The Fear of Feelings at Work," *The Atlantic*, May 1, 2017, https://www.theatlantic.com/business/archive/2017/05/feelings-at -work/524970.

Step Two: Apologize

1. Pumla Gobodo-Madikizela, *A Human Being Died That Night* (New York: Mariner Books, 2004).

2. Australian Government, "Apology to Australia's Indigenous Peoples," February 13, 2008, https://www.australia.gov.au/about-australia/our-country/ our-people/apology-to-australias-indigenous-peoples.

3. National Centre for Truth and Reconciliation, "About the National Centre for Truth and Reconciliation," University of Manitoba, http://nctr.ca/about-new.php.

4. Rob Capriccioso, "A Sorry Saga: Obama Signs Native American Apology Resolution; Fails to Draw Attention to It," Indian Law Resource Center, January 13, 2010, http://indianlaw.org/node/529.

5. Robert Beckford, *The Empire Pays Back*, BBC (2005). Available at https:// www.youtube.com/watch?v=MzctBXOHewk.

6. Peter Buffett, "Magic Words," https://www.peterbuffett.com/written -reflections/magic-words.

7. Hilary Giovale, interview by author, August 20, 2017.

8. Quoted in Edward J. Blum, *W. E. B. Du Bois, American Prophet* (Philadelphia: University of Pennsylvania Press, 2009).

9. The Times Editorial Board, "An Examination of The Times' Failures on Race, Our Apology and a Path Forward," *Los Angeles Times*, September 27, 2020, https://www.latimes.com/opinion/story/2020-09-27/ los-angeles-times-apology-racism.

10. American Library Association, "ALA Takes Responsibility for Past Racism, Pledges a More Equitable Association," press release, June 26, 2020, http:// www.ala.org/news/press-releases/2020/06/ala-takes-responsibility-past -racism-pledges-more-equitable-association.

11. Sara Lyons, interview by author, June 18, 2017.

12. Hilary Pearson et al., "The Philanthropic Community's Declaration of Action," *The Philanthropist*, June 15, 2015, https://thephilanthropist.ca/2015/06/the -philanthropic-communitys-declaration-of-action.

Step Three: Listen

1. Jennifer Buffett and Peter Buffett, interview by author, December 10, 2017.

2. Amber Nystrom, "How to Shut Up, and Other Lessons from the Godfather of Impact Investing—Jed Emerson," *Conscious Company* 10 (November/ December 2016), http://greenmoneyjournal.com/how-to-shut-up-and-other -lessons-from-the-godfather-of-impact-investing-jed-emerson.

3. Otto Scharmer and Katrin Kaufer, *Leading from the Emerging Future* (Oakland, CA: Berrett-Koehler Publishers, 2013).

4. J. David Goodman, "Amazon Pulls Out of Planned New York City Headquarters," *New York Times*, February 14, 2019, https://www.nytimes.com/2019/02/14/nyregion/amazon-hq2-queens.html.

5. Angel Enriquez, interview by author, August 10, 2020.

Step Four: Relate

1. Christopher Alexander, *The Timeless Way of Building* (Oxford: Oxford University Press, 1979).

2. Christopher Alexander, *The Nature of Order*, book 4, *The Luminous Ground* (London: Routledge, 2004).

3. Pamela Shifman, interview by author, August 10, 2017.

4. Yasmin Anwar, "Creating Love in the Lab: The 36 Questions That Spark Intimacy," *Berkeley News*, February 12, 2015, http://news.berkeley.edu/2015/02/12/love-in-the-lab.

5. Jeremy Heimans and Henry Timms, "Understanding 'New Power,'" *Harvard Business Review* (December 2014), https://hbr.org/2014/12/understanding-new-power.

6. Frederic Laloux, *Reinventing Organizations* (Brussels: Nelson Parker, 2014).

Step Five: Represent

1. Daryn Dodson, interview by author, December 3, 2017.

2. Bryan Stevenson, lecture at Yale Divinity School, February 1, 2017.

3. Gara LaMarche, interview by author, August 15, 2017.

4. Nevin Öztop, interview by author, August 3, 2017.

5. Nicole Richards, "The Door Is Open, We're Waiting for You to Walk through It," Australian Communities Foundation, https://communityfoundation.org.au/making-a-difference/stories/koondee-woonga-gat-toor-rong-john-harding.

6. "Neighborhood Strength: Creating a New Grantmaking Model in Crown Heights Brooklyn," Brooklyn Community Foundation, http://neighborhoods.brooklyncommunityfoundation.org.

7. Anna Clark, "Is Participatory Budgeting Real Democracy?," *Next City*, April 28, 2014, https://nextcity.org/features/view/is-participatory-budgeting-real-democracy-chicago.

8. Clark, "Is Participatory Budgeting Real Democracy?"

9. Jordan Flaherty, *No More Heroes: Grassroots Challenges to the Savior Mentality* (Oakland, CA: AK Press, 2016).

10. Caitlin Breedlove, "Willing to Be Transformed," *Medium*, September 24, 2015, https://medium.com/@caitlinbreedlove/willing-to-be-transformed-a-nine-year-queer-cross-race-work-marriage-33dd247d0bd5.

11. "Beyond Political Correctness: Building a Diverse Board," BoardSource, https://www.bridgespan.org/insights/library/boards/building-a-diverse-board.

12. Phillip Jackson, interview by author, August 26, 2017.

Step Six: Invest

1. Dana Arviso, interview by author, May 26, 2017.

2. Marc Gunther, "Where Do America's Big Foundations Invest Their Billions? Don't Ask," *Medium*, September 23, 2019, https://medium.com/nonprofit-chronicles/philanthropys-dark-money-2ed35022afc6.

3. Gregory Gethard, "Protest Divestment and the End of Apartheid," *Investopedia*, June 25, 2019, https://www.investopedia.com/articles/economics/08/protest-divestment-south-africa.asp.

4. Darren Walker, "Unleashing the Power of Endowments: The Next Great Challenge for Philanthropy," Ford Foundation, April 5, 2017, https://www.fordfoundation.org/ideas/equals-change-blog/posts/unleashing-the-power-of-endowments-the-next-great-challenge-for-philanthropy.

5. "The Evolution of Heron," F.B. Heron Foundation, http://www.heron.org/enterprise.

6. Stephen Huddart, interview by author, June 12, 2020.

7. "Investment Policy Statement (Updated December 2016)," F.B. Heron Foundation, December 5, 2016, https://www.heron.org/investment-policy-statement-updated-december-2016.

8. Amy Cortese, "For Impact Investor Kristin Hull, There Are Many Ways to Effect Change," *Locavesting*, May 9, 2017, https://www.locavesting.com/investing/for-impact-investor-kristin-hull-there-are-many-ways-to-effect-change.

9. Vanessa Daniel, "America Is Burning," *Medium*, September 13, 2017, https://medium.com/@GroundswellFund/americaisburning-4f154e201a3a.

Step Seven: Repair

1. Charles McGrath, "Global Foundation Assets Reach $1.5 Trillion," *Pensions & Investments*, May 8, 2018, https://www.pionline.com/article/20180508/INTERACTIVE/180509883/global-foundation-assets-reach-1-5-trillion.

2. "Global Assets under Management Set to Rise to $145.4 Trillion by 2025," PwC press release, October 30, 2017, https://press.pwc.com/News-releases/global-assets-under-management-set-to-rise-to--145.4-trillion-by-2025/s/e236a113-5115-4421-9c75-77191733f15f.

3. Rick Cohen, "Data Snapshot on Racial Justice Grantmaking," *Philanthropic Initiative for Racial Equity: Critical Issues* 5 (June 2014): 38.

4. Phillip Jackson, interview by author, August 26, 2017.

5. Zoe Mendelson, "In Chicago, a Case Study in the Ethics of Cultural Philanthropy," *Hyperallergic*, June 29, 2016, https://hyperallergic.com/308012/in-chicago-a-case-study-in-the-ethics-of-cultural-philanthropy.

6. Cheryl Heads, email to author, August 21, 2019.

7. According to the US SIF Foundation's 2016 *Report on US Sustainable, Responsible and Impact Investing Trends*, as of year-end 2015, more than one out of every five dollars under professional management in the United States—$8.72 trillion or more—was invested according to socially responsible investing strategies.

8. Richard F. America, "Reparations and Higher Education," *Diverse Issues in Higher Education*, January 7, 1999, http://diverseeducation.com/article/16.

9. Ta-Nehisi Coates, "The Case for Reparations," *The Atlantic*, June 2014, https://www.theatlantic.com/magazine/archive/2014/06/the-case-for-reparations/361631.

10. By September 2020, the list of foundations that had contributed assets to the Indigenous Resilience Fund included the All One Fund, the Counselling Foundation of Canada, Laidlaw Foundation, the Lawson Foundation, and the McConnell Foundation, as well as Toronto Foundation, Trottier Family Foundation, Vancity Community Investment Bank, Vancity Credit Union, and Suncor Energy Foundation. See "Indigenous Peoples Resilience Fund," Community Foundations of Canada, https://www.communityfoundations.ca/initiatives/indigenous-peoples-resilience-fund.

11. Stephen Huddart, interview by author, June 12, 2020.

12. "The Two Economies," Movement Net Lab, https://movementnetlab.org/living-resource-systems-a-new-approach-for-supporting-movement-networks.

13. Adam Simpson, Carla Skandier, and William A. Darity Jr., "For Reparations: A Conversation with William A. Darity Jr.," The Next System Project, March 10, 2017, https://thenextsystem.org/for-reparations.

14. Robert Pollin, James Heintz, and Thomas Herndon, "The Revenue Potential of a Financial Transaction Tax for U.S. Financial Markets," Political Economy Research Institute, University of Massachusetts at Amherst, July 30, 2017, https://www.peri.umass.edu/publication/item/698-the-revenue-potential-of-a-financial-transaction-tax-for-u-s-financial-markets.

15. Naomi Schaefer Riley, "One Way to Help Native Americans: Property Rights," *The Atlantic*, July 30, 2016, https://www.theatlantic.com/politics/archive/2016/07/native-americans-property-rights/492941.

16. Lawrence S. Bacow, "Initiative on Harvard and the Legacy of Slavery," Harvard University, Office of the President, November 21, 2019, https://www.harvard.edu/president/news/2019/initiative-on-harvard-and-legacy-slavery.

17. Tracy Scott Forson, "Enslaved Labor Built These Universities. Now They Are Starting to Repay the Debt," *USA Today*, February 12, 2020, https://eu.usatoday.com/story/news/education/2020/02/12/colleges-slavery-offering-atonement-reparations/2612821001.

18. Khorri Atkinson, "Reparations: Where the 2020 Democratic Candidates Stand," *Axios*, April 13, 2019, https://www.axios.com/reparations-2020-presidential-candidates-02cce9ac-082e-4777-955b-33c8196e64c0.html.

19. "Where Democrats Stand," *Washington Post*, https://www.washingtonpost.com/graphics/politics/policy-2020/economic-inequality/reparations/.

20. Associated Press, "Supreme Court Rules Swath of Oklahoma Remains Tribal Reservation," *NBC News*, July 9, 2020, https://www.nbcnews.com/politics/politics-news/supreme-court-rules-swath-oklahoma-remains-tribal-reservation-n1233315.

21. California State Lands Commission, "State Lands Commission Announces Return of Native American Tribal Land in Central California," June 23, 2020, https://www.slc.ca.gov/press-release/return-of-native-american-tribal-land-in-central-california.

22. Associated Press, "California Indian Tribe Gets Back Big Sur Ancestral Lands," *U.S. News & World Report*, July 28, 2020, https://www.usnews.com/news/best-states/california/articles/2020-07-28/california-indian-tribe-regains-part-of-ancestral-lands.

23. Simpson, Skandier, and Darity Jr., "For Reparations."

24. Rebecca Beitsch, "Judge Orders Mnuchin to Give Native American Tribes Full Stimulus Funding," *The Hill*, June 17, 2020, https://thehill.com/policy/energy-environment/503175-judge-orders-mnuchin-to-give-tribes-full-stimulus-funding.

25. Sahir Doshi, Allison Jordan, Kate Kelly, and Danyelle Solomon, "The COVID-19 Response in Indian Country: A Federal Failure," Center for American Progress, June 18, 2020, https://americanprogress.org/issues/green/reports/2020/06/18/486480/covid-19-response-indian-country.

Conclusion: Coming Full Circle

1. adrienne maree brown, *Emergent Strategy: Shaping Change, Changing Worlds* (Oakland, CA: AK Press, 2017).

2. Donna Chavis, interview by author, August 17, 2017.

3. Dana Arviso, interview by author, May 26, 2017.

4. David Graeber, "Army of Altruists," *Harper's*, January 2007, https://harpers.org/archive/2007/01/army-of-altruists.

5. Robin Wall Kimmerer, *Braiding Sweetgrass: Indigenous Wisdom, Scientific Knowledge, and the Teachings of Plants* (Minneapolis: Milkweed Editions, 2013), 165.

6. Iyuskin American Horse, "'We Are Protectors, not Protesters': Why I'm Fighting the North Dakota Pipeline," *Guardian*, August 18, 2016, https://www.theguardian.com/us-news/2016/aug/18/north-dakota-pipeline-activists-bakken-oil-fields.

7. Camille Seaman, "Gallery: Portraits from the Standing Rock Protests," Ideas. TED.com, November 9, 2016, https://ideas.ted.com/gallery-portraits-from-the-standing-rock-protests.

8. Morgan Guyton, "Decolonizing Christianity with Alicia Crosby and AnaYelsi Velasco-Sanchez," Crackers and Grape Juice podcast, episode 61, posted on Patheos, December 13, 2016, http://www.patheos.com/blogs/mercynotsacrifice/2016/12/13/decolonizing-christianity-alicia-crosby-anayelsi-velasco-sanchez.

9. Dr. Rupa Marya, Facebook post, Spring 2016.

10. Donna Chavis, interview by author, August 17, 2017.

11. Desmond Tutu, *The Book of Forgiving* (San Francisco: HarperOne, 2014).

Glossary of New Terms

colonizer virus: What remains in society, culture, and institutions after the conquest phase of colonization is done; the compelling tactics of division, control, and exploitation. Nowhere is the virus more present than in how we deal with wealth.

donor fragility: The fear of talking to wealthy, privileged donors about issues of race or power out of fear of losing their support.

global bleaching: The side effect of colonizers traveling the earth to consolidate wealth—a staggering reduction in the number of religions, languages, species, cultures, social systems, media channels, political systems, and so on. The result is a more bland and boring world that is less innovative and less resilient.

ivory towers: Institutions that maintain the white supremacist culture and operate according to the colonizer mantra of "Divide, control, exploit."

listening in color: The combination of listening openly without controlling the parameters of what can be said, listening with empathy and allowing the experiences of the speaker to permeate, and listening for what is being said beyond the words spoken.

loans-to-gifts spectrum: The collection of institutions that control access to wealth, from banks to investment firms to foundations; collectively also called "funders."

medicine money: Resources and wealth used intentionally to heal divides and restore balance to the earth.

orphans: A compassionate term for non-Indigenous people of all backgrounds, indicating the severing from their ancestral territories and their ancient ways (with thanks to Stephen Jenkinson).

shiny new penny syndrome: An aspect of internalized oppression, when a new person of color threatens the existing token person of color's position of power.

Whitney Houston–Bobby Brown syndrome: An aspect of internalized oppression in which you have to diminish yourself in order to not steal the spotlight of someone else at your organization who has more power than you.

Discussion Guide and Resources

Discussion Guide

Part One: Where It Hurts

1. Philanthropists are often accused of searching for answers with their right hand to problems they had created or contributed to with their left. How do you think this dynamic manifests itself, and how can people with wealth address it?

2. What are the barriers that make it difficult for communities of color to benefit from philanthropy or other resources or opportunities? What have you observed in your own work? What are some of the ways you can change your practices to be more equitable?

3. Villanueva writes that the Lumbee Indians' first question when meeting someone new is "Who's your people?" Who are your people, and how have they been affected by colonialism, historically and today? How do you think this history shapes your relationship to wealth?

Part Two: Being a Healer

4. In the Indigenous worldview, many kinds of things can be medicine. Anyone can find and use medicine, just by allowing your intuition and feelings to determine whether something can serve as medicine. What is your medicine?

5. Beyond philanthropy and finance, what sectors do you think are most ready for decolonization? Where might they begin?

6. In this section, Villanueva speaks to the power of "story" as medicine. What is the power in your story and how can you share it?

Part Three: How to Heal

7. Villanueva outlines seven steps to healing our relationship to wealth: grieve, apologize, listen, relate, represent, invest, and repair. How do you think you can undertake this process in your own relationship to wealth?

8. How might investors, philanthropic and nonprofit organizations, and businesses work to decolonize wealth?

9. Which particular step to healing are you most interested in activating?

10. What are the specific barriers you envision needing to overcome? Personally? In your workplace, business, or philanthropy?

11. What is the boldest step you're willing to take today toward decolonizing wealth?

Additional Resources from the Author

Join Liberated Capital

Liberated Capital supports Indigenous and other people-of-color-led initiatives working for transformative social change. This fund—directed by the Decolonizing Wealth Project—aims to move untethered resources to help shape a future in which we can all heal from generations of colonial trauma and thrive in our cultures.

Rooted in relationships of mutuality and equity, Liberated Capital gives through a reparations model that trusts and supports the leadership of those most impacted by historical and systemic racism. The fund welcomes support from individuals at all levels of giving who are committed to collectively healing the wounds of colonialism and white supremacy by using money as medicine to shape an equitable future.

Join us in supporting a fund that can help us all be courageous in moving resources together, undertaking the long process of healing required to restore balance so that all communities can flourish.

Money as Medicine: *A Guided Journal for Reflection and Action*

This journal is a resource for decolonizing wealth and using money as medicine for healing and wholeness. It will provide you with practical guidance to take action based on the central insights of *Decolonizing Wealth*, the Seven Steps to Healing, and ways to use your "medicine" at home, at work, and in your community. It will give you opportunities to reflect on your relationship to money, racial justice, and the history of colonization in the United States, and its global implications, and to identify practical action steps toward reconciliation. This journal is for everyone.

You've read *Decolonizing Wealth* and you're ready for more. *Money as Medicine* is designed for you.

Download the Decolonizing Wealth Toolkit

The Decolonizing Wealth Toolkit is a free digital resource to support your journey as a past, present, or future reader of Decolonizing Wealth. Find it at **decolonizingwealth.com/thetoolkit**.

DecolonizingWealth.com

Acknowledgments

Thanks to the Creator and to my sweet mother, Sheila Jacobs. Thanks, Mama, for your unconditional love and for teaching me the spirit of giving and generosity of the heart. And to the rest of my family: thank you for always finding a good laugh, even in the face of adversity. I love you.

Eternal gratitude to my chosen family—the loves of my life and my soul mates—for your support during this project and in life in general: Will Cordery, Mayra Alvarez Sparacino, Sadye Paez, Michelle Ramos Lopez, Yesenia Polanco, Tricia Levesque, Chris Locklear, Chris Lee, and Tenney Farmer.

The following philanthropists, advocates, leaders, and all-around good folks provided insights and wisdom to this work:

Andrea Armeni, Dana Arviso, Tamieka Atkins, Rod Brown, Ryan Bowers, Kelly Brown, Jennifer and Peter Buffett, David Callahan, Chris Cardona, Agnes Chavis, Donna Chavis, William Cordery, Aaron Dorfman, Farhad A. Ebrahimi, Angel Enriquez, Kwabena Allen Frimpong, Jose A. Garcia, Hilary Giovale, Gita Gulati-Partee, Tracie D. Hall, Carly Hare, Melissa Johnson Hewitt, Stephen Huddart, Phillip Jackson, Camille Kalama, Elizabeth Krause, Gara LaMarche, Melinda Maynor Lowery, Sara Lyons, Nevin Öztop, Leticia Peguero, Tia Oros Peters, Andre Perez, Cynthia Renfro, Tricia Stevens, Pamela Shifman, Christi Tran, and Dorian Warren.

Thanks also to:

- My team at Decolonizing Wealth Project, Tricia Levesque and Cara Venter, for holding me down and for being on this whirlwind journey with me.

- The team at Berrett-Koehler Publishers, especially my editor, Steve Piersanti, all of whom have been huge cheerleaders from the start of our relationship.

- The Lumbee Tribe of North Carolina—my people—for keeping me grounded. Healing is our path to liberation!

- To my philanthropic elders—the leaders of color who came before me and coached and loved me—I stand on your shoulders: Susan Taylor Batten, Angela Glover Blackwell, Donna Chavis, Louis Delgado, Linetta Gilbert, Susan Jenkins, Valorie Johnson, Peggy Saika, Gladys Washington, to name a few.

- To everyone who has worked with me in any way—I'm better off because of you. There are too many names to list, but thank you.

- Last but not least, my dear friend Ariane Conrad, the Book Doula. You are still the most brilliant (and patient) person I've ever met. Who could have imagined this journey!? I can't wait to see where we'll go next!

Index

About the Author

From an early age, Edgar Villanueva knew he would devote himself to ministry, to medicine, to being of service. He earned a bachelor of arts degree from Jackson College of Ministries and a bachelor of science in public health and a master's degree in health care administration from the University of North Carolina's Gillings School of Global Public Health. Ultimately, he  found his way to philanthropy, the field named for the love of humankind, where for the past 16 years he has given away tens of millions of dollars each year, mostly to low-income communities across the United States.

Today, Edgar is a best-selling author, activist, and frequent keynote speaker at conferences around the world, where he regularly inspires engagement in the Seven Steps to Healing. In 2018, Edgar released his first book, *Decolonizing Wealth*, which offers hopeful and compelling alternatives to the dynamics of colonization in the philanthropic and social finance sectors.

Edgar is also the founder and principal of the Decolonizing Wealth Project and of Liberated Capital, a nonprofit and a fund that envision a world where racial equity has become a societal norm—where new systems ensure that everyone can live their best lives, thrive in their cultures, and heal from generations of colonial trauma. He also advises high-net-worth individuals, philanthropists, and global institutions on allocating resources more equitably.

Edgar consults with national and global philanthropies, Fortune 500 corporations, and nonprofits on powerful but practical opportunities to advance racial equity inside their institutions and through their investment strategies. His work has been featured in various media outlets, including the *New York Times*, *Washington Post*, *Vox*, and NPR.

Edgar is proud to be an enrolled member of the Lumbee Tribe of North Carolina as well as a Southerner, lineages from which he inherited the love of storytelling and his strong devotion to community. His Native name, Niigaanii Beneshi (Ojibwe), means "Leading Bird," signifying the bird at the front of the flock when it flies in V formation, the bird that bears the full brunt of the wind and sets the pace for the rest. Much of the inspiration for the "medicine" prescribed in the pages of *Decolonizing Wealth* comes from Native elders and the Indigenous worldview.

As is true of most Lumbee Indians, faith has been a major influence in Edgar's life. The church gave Edgar's early years a stability and purpose that he firmly believes is the reason why he's made it as far as he has. Over the years, his faith has evolved but not wavered. He holds fast to traditions he believes to be valuable.

His chosen family includes the advocates and activists who are engaged in the struggle for racial justice, civil rights, and human rights. They celebrate birthdays and weddings together; they comfort each other in the face of violence and bigotry. Their professional is their personal.

Poverty and wealth; Native, Southern, and Christian traditions; ministry, health care, activism, and philanthropy. Braiding these many threads together gives Edgar his unique perspective on decolonization, the process of recovering from trauma, and the potential for money to help humanity heal.

He has held leadership roles on numerous boards and advisory committees, at organizations such as the Andrus Family Fund, Native Americans in Philanthropy, NDN Collective, and *Mother Jones*. Edgar has been a Hull Fellow with the Southeastern Council of Foundations and a fellow with the American College of Healthcare Executives. More recently, Edgar was an Atlantic Fellow for Racial Equity and a Civil Society Fellow.

In June 2014, Edgar was awarded the Flying Eagle Woman award from Native Americans in Philanthropy, recognizing his many years in community-led, culturally inspired leadership. It was an apt recognition of the Leading Bird. In 2019, *Inside Philanthropy* named him the Most Radical Critic of Philanthropy, and in 2020 he was named an Angelic Troublemaker by Ozy Media. Follow Edgar on Twitter and Instagram at @VillanuevaEdgar.

Berrett–Koehler
Publishers

Berrett-Koehler is an independent publisher dedicated to an ambitious mission: *Connecting people and ideas to create a world that works for all.*

Our publications span many formats, including print, digital, audio, and video. We also offer online resources, training, and gatherings. And we will continue expanding our products and services to advance our mission.

We believe that the solutions to the world's problems will come from all of us, working at all levels: in our society, in our organizations, and in our own lives. Our publications and resources offer pathways to creating a more just, equitable, and sustainable society. They help people make their organizations more humane, democratic, diverse, and effective (and we don't think there's any contradiction there). And they guide people in creating positive change in their own lives and aligning their personal practices with their aspirations for a better world.

And we strive to practice what we preach through what we call "The BK Way." At the core of this approach is *stewardship,* a deep sense of responsibility to administer the company for the benefit of all of our stakeholder groups, including authors, customers, employees, investors, service providers, sales partners, and the communities and environment around us. Everything we do is built around stewardship and our other core values of *quality, partnership, inclusion,* and *sustainability.*

This is why Berrett-Koehler is the first book publishing company to be both a B Corporation (a rigorous certification) and a benefit corporation (a for-profit legal status), which together require us to adhere to the highest standards for corporate, social, and environmental performance. And it is why we have instituted many pioneering practices (which you can learn about at www.bkconnection.com), including the Berrett-Koehler Constitution, the Bill of Rights and Responsibilities for BK Authors, and our unique Author Days.

We are grateful to our readers, authors, and other friends who are supporting our mission. We ask you to share with us examples of how BK publications and resources are making a difference in your lives, organizations, and communities at www.bkconnection.com/impact.

Dear reader,

Thank you for picking up this book and welcome to the worldwide BK community! You're joining a special group of people who have come together to create positive change in their lives, organizations, and communities.

What's BK all about?

Our mission is to connect people and ideas to create a world that works for all.

Why? Our communities, organizations, and lives get bogged down by old paradigms of self-interest, exclusion, hierarchy, and privilege. But we believe that can change. That's why we seek the leading experts on these challenges—and share their actionable ideas with you.

A welcome gift

To help you get started, we'd like to offer you a **free copy** of one of our bestselling ebooks:

www.bkconnection.com/welcome

When you claim your **free ebook**, you'll also be subscribed to our blog.

Our freshest insights

Access the best new tools and ideas for leaders at all levels on our blog at ideas.bkconnection.com.

Sincerely,

Your friends at Berrett-Koehler